LOVE
IN THE
PALM
OF YOUR
HAND

LOVE
IN THE
PALM
OF YOUR
HAND

HOW TO USE
PALMISTRY
FOR SUCCESSFUL
RELATIONSHIPS

Ghanshyam Singh Birla

Destiny Books
Rochester, Vermont

Destiny Books
One Park Street
Rochester, Vermont 05767
Destiny Books is a division of Inner Traditions International
www.InnerTraditions.com

Library of Congress Cataloging-in-Publication Data
Birla, Ghanshyam Singh, 1941–
Love in the palm of your hand : how to use palmistry for
successful relationships / Ghanshyam Singh Birla.
p.   cm.
Includes index.
ISBN 0-89281-718-6 (pbk. : alk. paper)
1. Palmistry. 2. Love. I. Title.
BF935.L67B57   1998
133.6—dc21   98-38310
                                            CIP

Printed and bound in Canada

10   9   8   7   6   5   4   3   2   1

Original artwork by Sophie Bisaillon
Text design and layout by Virginia L. Scott
This book was typeset in Goudy

Dedicated to Mother Panchanguli, Goddess of Samudrik Shastra.

Her inspiration has provided me with the privilege of examining many thousands of pairs of hands over the last three decades. If it were not for them, I would never have been able to gather and share with you the pearls of wisdom from the ancient art and science of Samudrik Shastra—the ocean of knowledge from which palmistry was born.

Contents

Acknowledgments

Working with love in the company of loving souls for the ultimate enrichment of Love in all human hearts has proven to be a rare and blessed task.

Love is said to be synonymous with God, the only real substance. It is for this reason, perhaps, that Swami Vivekananda, an exalted disciple of Ramakrishna Paramahamsa, said, "In the conflict between the head and the heart, follow the heart." Ancient Hindu scriptures confirm that God's dwelling place is the human heart.

This book is the product of many loving hearts and a labor of love for many souls. I am thankful to all those souls who rendered their hearts to me by allowing me to peek into the chambers from whence flow the heart lines—the chambers where *sat*, the only real substance and the essence of *sattwa*, resides. Their generous permission to use their hand prints for the inspiration of others is gratefully acknowledged.

I am also grateful for the support and encouragement of many precious longtime friends, especially Mary Stark, whose invaluable editing and research over the years has contributed a great deal to this work. I would also like to express special gratitude to Adel Bichara, and to Pierre Saint-Cyr, who believed in this project from the very start.

To all the volunteers and students at the National Research Institute for Self Understanding (N.R.I.S.U.), whose dedicated spirit of serving through the discipline of palmistry has allowed me to benefit my research, I am truly thankful.

For the conception, nurturance, and finally the birth of *Love in the Palm of Your Hand*, I feel very privileged to have received the support of, and am therefore grateful to:

—my late grandparents, Shri Naitram Singh Birla and Smt Paimanya Devi Birla, who sowed the seed of aspiration in my heart, at the very tender age of twelve, to explore the ancient arts and sciences of *jyotish* and *Samudrik Shastra*.

—my late loving parents, Shri Nain Singh Birla and Smt Antvanti Devi Birla, who allowed me to walk in the footsteps of my grandfather's quest for wisdom.

—all my loving teachers in the arts and sciences of Vedic astrology, palmistry, mantra, meditation, and related spiritual sciences, especially to the late Pdt Shyam Lal Ji, whose benign grace and insightful revelations continue to throb in my heart to this day.

—my uncle, Mamaji Shri Kirin Pal Singh, who was greatly instrumental in enriching my research by his loving dedication to securing many hand prints at a very early stage.

—all my early students, superior officers, professors, and colleagues in the Ministry of Education, Government of India, whose permission to analyze the morphological features of their hands and feet gave me the confidence to classify specific traits, including strengths, weaknesses, and areas of particular expertise.

—my very loving friend and teaching colleague of the late '60s, Navin Kumar Goel, and his family, to whom I am eternally indebted for their encouragement to stabilize my role as a personal growth consultant in Delhi, and secondly for wholeheartedly supporting my research aptitude in palmistry in the multicultural society of Montreal.

—my brothers and sisters in India, who endured a great deal of my exhaustless passion for peering into the hearts of many through their hands and feet.

—my loving and dedicated wife Chanchala, devoted mother and teacher of our children, together with whom I have had the opportunity over the past thirty years of testing many of the practical suggestions offered in this book, without whose patience, support, and understanding I would never have been able to initiate this project.

—my beloved sons Keero and Abhishekananda, and especially my loving daughter Rekha, whose initial inspiration to produce a self-help audiocassette on how to grow a positive heart line served as a stepping-stone to the book itself.

—the late Judy Freppel, who perceived the importance of palmistry in depicting human potentials so much that she left her position as psychologist at a rehabilitation center in Montreal and hastened to cofound the N.R.I.S.U. with mutual friends Elaine and Grant Clark to promote Vedic palmistry and astrology in Montreal.

—my student, friend, and colleague Kathleen Keogh, palmist, astrologer, and vice-president of N.R.I.S.U. since 1978, who has proven to be a rare instrument of Mother Panchanguli. Her very inquisitive nature along with objective reasoning and devotion to palmistry has enabled her to systematize all the courses given at our center from introductory to advanced levels under my guidance. Kathleen's undying commitment to present a work that describes the heart line in unparalleled precision and depth has brought this project to fruition.

—Peter Keogh, palmist and astrologer of many years at N.R.I.S.U., who, in collaboration with his sister Kathleen, worked with steadfast dedication and creative ingenuity to provide a solid structure to the book.

—my very precious friend Patricia Munro Conway, Dean of English at Vanier College, without whose chief editorial help this book would not have been completed.

—my very treasured friends and colleagues at the Palmistry Center. "Production Team Unit I": my son Keero Birla for his expertise in computer design, Sophie Bisaillon for her excellent and original artwork, Guylaine Vallée for her uncommon enthusiasm in tireless research and hand print scanning, Nazneen Wallis for her ardent zeal and perspicacity in typing, editing, and proofreading, Chandan Rugenius for his ingenious assistance at all levels of production, and Johanne Riopel for her computer art excellence. "Second Unit" staff members of the production team: Marie-Claire Sauvé, Heather Flockhart, Denise Parisé, Jacinthe Côté, Rémi Riverin, Elyise Trépanier, and Grace Macklin. For their sincere moral support I am especially indebted.

—my unique friend Pasquali Roberto, Astrologer, for his many years of inspiration and continuous support of the discipline of palmistry, and especially for demonstrating the positive growth of his own heart line at will, upon my recommendation.

—all my clients who initially came to me as skeptics and returned as the greatest advocates of palmistry.

—my old-time client, friend, and agent Dianne Thomas, whose initial "Can Do" slogan motivated me to take concrete steps to broaden the horizons of publication of the book.

—my publisher, Inner Traditions, whose love at first sight of the manuscript has brought this book to your hands. I bow to their noble ideal of bringing "soul awareness" to the world through their publications.

—and last but not least, I am sincerely indebted to my Guru, Paramahansa Yoganandaji, for strengthening the spark of introspection within me and inspiring me to ignite the same in all human hearts, so that one day we can all usher our consciousness into the Divine Love of All Love—God Himself.

Preface

We all recognize that the first and foremost requirement for happiness is love—human and divine. But what is the nature of love? Where do we find it? How may we nurture it? And can it be repaired, if broken?

The ancient *rishis* of India confirmed, through thousands of years of empirical observation, that every aspect of human life—physical, psychological, emotional, and spiritual—is reflected in the lines and signs of the hands. However, the features of the hand, unlike our skin or eye color, are not fixed genetically. As we see in upcoming chapters, the hands are able to signal possible positive events in our lives as well as provide warnings about negative tendencies that may lead to difficulty. Over centuries, palmistry has been used as a means of counseling and as a tool in the acquisition of self-knowledge. With understanding and self-awareness comes the capability to exercise our will to learn from past mistakes and, by resolving them now, alter tendencies that may lead to future difficulty. We can learn to use the study of palmistry, then, as our guide to developing loving relationships.

This book was written in response to the growing needs of many clients, friends, and students over the past three decades of my practice. The search for love and the mending of fractured relationships is of primary concern to virtually everyone. With the inspiration, encouragement, and support of my family and friends, it is now my privilege to offer the reader this guide to building successful human relationships.

The information presented here is based on actual lifelong practice and research. Primarily concerned with how to discover love and nurture it, this book provides an overview of palmistry, as well as explanatory hand prints, illustrations, and case histories. A detailed study of the heart line in relation to the other lines and signs of the hand allows us to find our own particular configuration, and hence our own approach to love in all its aspects.

It is my heartfelt wish that you are inspired to develop deep and loving relationships through the help of this book. It is with this purpose that I offer you *Love in the Palm of Your Hand*.

About the Author

Born in 1941 in Uttar Pradesh, India, Ghanshyam Singh Birla cofounded the Montreal-based National Research Institute for Self-Understanding in 1972.

Dr. Birla teaches, consults, and writes on a variety of subjects including astrology, palmistry, gem, mantra, magnet, and cosmic ray therapy. In 1996 he received an Honorary Ph.D. from the Council of Alternative Systems of Medicine, Calcutta, India, in recognition of his ongoing work to promote alternative therapies. *Love in the Palm of Your Hand* is Dr. Birla's first book.

Introduction

Each one of us longs for deep and meaningful relationships. In a lifetime we have numerous opportunities to experience a union of souls: between business associates, friends, a parent and child, a husband and wife, a teacher and student, a guru and disciple.

We come together—consciously or subconsciously—to help each other fulfill a purpose. We have a choice. Either we can enter into a relationship fully aware of the impact the union is likely to have on us, or we can enter into one oblivious to what we may be about to set in motion.

What Do We Mean by a Loving Relationship?

In Sanskrit, the language of the Vedas, the term that best approximates "relationship" is *sambandh*, which derives from *sam*, meaning whole, and *bandh*, meaning bound. Within this word lies a paradox. In order to be whole, free, fully realized beings we must choose to be bound—to be connected—whether to ourself or to another. And these bonds, these connections, allow us to move forward in freedom.

This binding force permeates the entire universe. It exists in every atom of creation. The Moon is bound to the Earth, just as the Earth is bound to the Sun; so also protons, electrons, and neutrons are bound together to form atoms. Therefore, the binding force exists in each one of us—in the very fabric of our physical body. This universal interconnectedness was understood by the ancient *rishis* (sages) of India, who developed a system of interpreting the features of the human body, one branch of which was palmistry.

1

What Is Palmistry?

Palmistry is the study of the lines and signs of the hands. Throughout our lifetime, our bodies register change. For example, the lines on our face that we acquire with age reflect experience and, we hope, wisdom. Lines and signs on our hands, present at birth, grow as we evolve, signifying the accumulated experience of our lives.

Centuries ago, the sages of India established a system of knowledge stemming from the Vedas, the earliest sacred Hindu scriptures. They studied the hands as a means to unveil and understand the self and relationships with others. They saw that the unique patterns of lines and signs in the hand come into being as a direct result of the way we think. Just as a pebble thrown into the water creates ripples, so our thoughts create similar effects.

Our hands offer us an objective view of who we really are. Through the study of palmistry, we have the opportunity to see to what extent our thoughts and feelings influence our happiness and the harmony of those around us. As we exercise our will in choosing positive patterns of thinking to replace any negative ones, we see our lines begin to change, reflecting a shift in our consciousness. As Shakespeare observed, we are masters of our own fate, that "the fault . . . is not in our stars, but in ourselves."

How Do We Use Palmistry to Find Love?

The sages of India observed over time that specific physical features of the hands alter in response to changes in our physiological, intellectual, and emotional makeup.

For example, a nine-year-old boy who blamed himself for his parents' divorce showed a head line with a clearly discernible break where none had been evident before. This break reflected his inability to comprehend the dissolution of his family. However, it would be misleading to interpret the significance of the lines of head, heart, destiny, and so on in isolation from the whole hand. The child also had a strong heart line, indicating the inner resources to survive this traumatic experience. Hand prints taken several years later showed the break beginning to repair.

It is the pattern of lines, then, not the individual lines themselves, that is significant. The boy's long heart line signified his ability to feel deeply. However, he had a choice. He could have allowed negative feelings to overwhelm him and make him bitter—first toward his parents, then in his own dealings with others. Instead, he overcame his pain and learned to recognize that human relationships are complex; he became forgiving and compassionate. In his adult life, he was able to develop healthy bonds with others. In fact, it was a dialogue between the intellect being able to recognize human frailty and the heart being able to accept it with understanding that brought about the transformation both in the lines of the hand and in the young man.

The process of forming a bond with another person is analogous to going for a drive in the country. We can venture forth with no goal in mind, and take whatever country lanes or woodland roads seem attractive. We may have the adventure of a lifetime, or we may become completely lost. However, with a map, we can still choose the interesting fork in the road; but we will always know where we are and where we are going. Palmistry is the roadmap we consult on our journey through life. The study of the features of the hand with its lines and signs allows us to see where we are physically, emotionally, intellectually, and spiritually. We can also see the direction we are likely to take—unless we choose otherwise. The map of the hand shows us possible obstacles and impediments to our progress, which we can either avoid or transform.

1
Your Hands: A Personal Blueprint

THE STUDY OF PALMISTRY

Centuries ago, the sages of India transcribed the wisdom of the Vedas into six major texts known as Vedangas (or limbs of the Vedas). One of the foremost of these limbs—*jyotish*—represents the "eyes" of the Vedas. Jyotish, which translates literally as lord of light, is the study of the effects of light on human beings—in particular, the heavenly lights of Sun, Moon, stars, and planets.

Jyotish itself contains many branches of learning. One of them, Samudrik Shastra, which translates as the ocean of knowledge, consists of a system of interpreting the features of the human body (human morphology). Just as the Earth is part of the solar system, which is part of the Milky Way galaxy—itself, merely a small part of the universe—so each of us is a microcosmic universe with galaxies, constellations, and solar systems. Each cell with its protons, neutrons, and electrons is a miniature solar system. The human body is constructed in patterns that repeat themselves down to the microscopic level. For example, we can see that the circulatory system, with its multiple-scale branching arteries, veins, capillaries, and blood vessels, repeats the same pattern from large to small. The configuration of lines on the hand follows a similar design of multiscale branching.

Within Samudrik Shastra there are many branches of knowledge, such as graphology (the study of handwriting), phrenology (the study of the structure of the

5

skull), and palmistry. In India, palmistry is known as hast jyotish, which is the study of the effects of light from the heavenly bodies on *hast*—the hand.

To a greater or lesser degree, most people experience physiological reactions to emotions. Our hands turn cold and clammy before a visit to the dentist, we blush when praised or embarrassed, our throat tightens when we hear that a loved one has been stricken with calamity, and laughter releases tension. There is an observable link between the mind and body. The mind may function consciously or subliminally. In the East, this observed link between mind and body extends to the hand. The rishis say that as an individual evolves through life the lines and patterns of the hands change; and consistently, modifications appear in particular lines reflecting positive or negative changes in specific areas of human life. Over centuries, the science of palmistry developed into a method for developing self-awareness.

Just as our dread of the dentist's chair makes our heart palpitate, so our thought patterns and mental preoccupations form the details of lines in our hands. The quality of these lines and signs is in direct proportion to our level of consciousness. In other words, we ourselves program the details seen in our hands whether we are conscious of this or not.

SELF-AWARENESS THROUGH PALMISTRY

The goal of palmistry is to assist personal evolution by establishing an equilibrium in all areas of life through greater self-awareness. This equilibrium can be cultivated at the conscious, subconscious, and superconscious levels. A better understanding of the three levels of awareness will help you gain insight into your own reactions to everyday life situations, including your relationships.

The Three Levels of Awareness

The Hindu scriptures teach that each of us is essentially a soul. According to the Vedas, the physical body that we can see and touch is only one of our three bodies. It is interpenetrated by a second with a higher and finer rate of vibration, the astral body—the refined energy template that gives rise to the physical body. The physical body is structured and maintained according to the specifications of the astral body. The third body, known as the causal body, has an even subtler rate of vibration than the other two. It forms the true basis of the person's being—the "cause" or original blueprint—and carries forward, in altered form, from one lifetime to the next. In the study of hast jyotish, when we look into the hand, we are really looking at the astral and causal bodies through their reflection in the physical body.

The conscious mind, parallel to the physical body, works with the five senses: sight, hearing, smell, taste, and touch. It functions when we are awake and is inactive during sleep. The subconscious mind, however, which parallels the astral body, never sleeps, as it is constantly monitoring life-support systems such as the heart, brain, and lungs. Further, during our waking hours, the subconscious continually records impressions that underlie the information picked up through our senses; these impressions are then replayed at night in our dreams.

In Eastern texts, the superconscious mind, which parallels the causal body, is referred to as *atma* or soul. It is the light of pure consciousness.

The science of jyotish (the study of the effects of light) was developed to bring understanding as to how each of us filters this soul light through our subconscious and conscious minds. Through the study of jyotish, we can learn how to refract the personalized color spectrum that is our individuality back through the prism of the mind to rediscover the original source of light, which is our true heritage.

The superconscious is pure energy and speaks to us most clearly through our intuition. The ordinary conscious mind, which operates through the five physical senses, is finite as it is confined to operating within a transitory physical body and, thus, subject to the laws of relativity. The superconscious mind, however, is infinite and not limited to the rules governing the physical body.

Depending on our level of evolutionary development, we have varying degrees of awareness of the conscious mind in the awakened state, and of the subconscious mind through our dreams. We can also, over time, become aware of the superconscious mind or soul. The soul can speak to us through the medium of the subconscious mind, which in turn relays its message to the conscious.

As the five senses are kept occupied by a constant barrage of data, it is difficult to hear the whispers of the soul. Fortunately, we have a built-in system to access and make sense of the subtle nuances of this higher mind. When we sleep, the conscious senses are temporarily stilled, enabling us to enter into a realm not confined by time and space. The subconscious mind is thus freed to "televise" the subtle messages of the superconscious through dreams. How accurately these soul messages come through usually depends on the quality and level of our waking consciousness.

During the day the conscious mind may be preoccupied, anxious, or simply busy with the complexities of the external environment. During sleep, we carry this static into our dreams, distorting whatever messages the superconscious is trying to convey to us through the medium of the subconscious.

Alternatively, if we are able to maintain a sense of peace and calm during our waking hours, such static is eliminated. The more we learn to calm the conscious mind, to observe, and to respond, rather than blindly react to events, the more we alter the ratio between signal and noise in our favor, which in turn allows us to hear better whatever message is being sent. Rather than being a composite of random and disjointed thoughts and events, dreams become a medium through which the purity of the superconscious—that is, the soul—can speak to us and be clearly understood. Our dreams can become enlightening, perhaps even visionary.

This is not to say that you have to wait until you sleep to connect with this source that reflects the true inner self. The subconscious serves as an interface helping to introduce the superconscious to the conscious; once you have increased your waking awareness and learned to realign all three levels of your consciousness, you can begin to draw upon the superconscious while in a conscious state.

Through this heightened awareness, you gain a true perspective of reality. Although this connection doesn't happen overnight, it is comforting to think that with time and effort you can access this level. Working through jyotish, you can learn to recognize a deeper aspect of the self. The process itself is a path, and the relationships you attract while on it contribute to your growth and happiness.

The Gunas: An Eastern Approach to the Three Levels of Awareness

In the East, the three levels of consciousness are represented by the three *gunas,* or qualities of nature—*sattwa, rajas,* and *tamas.* Everything in the universe is influenced in whole or in part by these three complementary threads found woven throughout nature. The conscious, subconscious, and superconscious minds relate to tamas, rajas, and sattwa respectively.

Sattwa refers to everything that enlightens and is positively (+) charged. Tamas is a negatively (-) charged force whose nature is to obscure and darken; it is essential because it creates form. The soul enters the physical body courtesy of the tamas force. Once in the body, the soul is continuously challenged to struggle against the consistent downward-pulling force of gravity, which is the hallmark of tamas. It is for this reason that tamas is considered an obstructing force and, in nature, is considered dense.

Rajas, the pivotal force of this triad, is neutral. It is simply a fulcrum upon which sattwa and tamas perform their roles so that we can ultimately attain an equilibrium in our lives. These forces are ceaselessly at work and are perceived in the entirety of the human condition, for example, as pain and pleasure, love and hate, or good and bad.

The physical body is born into this world fully equipped with the five senses, and it is due

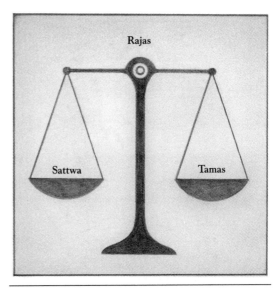

Rajas acts as a fulcrum upon which sattwa *and* tamas *perform their roles so that we can ultimately attain an equilibrium in our lives.*

to the senses that the body is considered tamas. This is primarily because we, as individuals, are generally not in control of our senses and the various impulses, desires, and attachments associated with them. So, although it is essential for human life and for the evolution of consciousness, the body may become a tremendous liability, making it difficult for us to attain the equilibrium we are inherently striving for.

If you are to find this balance, it becomes a necessity to embrace sattwic qualities such as peace, conscientiousness, and unconditional love, to name a few. It is a matter of learning to trust your intuition and your soul—or superconscious—within which is a powerful sattwic force of light.

Rajas, which means king, relates to the mind. In its unique position as an interface between the soul and body, it has the ability to unify the three gunas or to keep them isolated from each other. The true power of the mind lies in its ability to become the perfect medium through which the light of sattwa can illuminate, integrate, and refine the tamas of the physical body.

In the *Bhagavad Gita*, Krishna tells Arjuna, "The mind can become our greatest friend or worst enemy." Ultimately, it is up to the mind to realize a sense of integration within or to keep us occupied in the world of duality with its never-ending cycles of pain and pleasure.

Once you have learned to integrate the three gunas (or levels of awareness), you become whole, complete, and in harmony.

The three gunas, interwoven in nature throughout the universe, are also present in the micro-universe of the hand. The palm is divided into sattwa, rajas, and tamas. Each section, or mount, of the hand is also subdivided into sattwa, rajas, and tamas. And, in turn, each section of the mount is divided into the three gunas and so forth.

The Three Levels of Consciousness Seen in the Hand

Within your palm, you can see the interplay of these three gunas, or levels of consciousness. The mounts (Luna, Venus, Mars, Jupiter, Saturn, Sun, Mercury, Rahu, and Ketu) represent individualized fragments of the superconscious. The major lines (heart, head, and life) correspond to your subconscious level of awareness. The minor lines (destiny, Sun, Mercury, and so on) represent your conscious ability to mine the richness of the hidden subconscious and superconscious energies within you.

If you think of the hand as a map of the mind, then the hills and valleys of the mounts are its terrain—the living soil of your supercon-

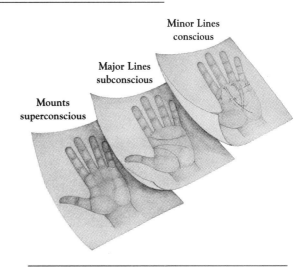

Minor Lines conscious

Major Lines subconscious

Mounts superconscious

The three levels of consciousness seen in the hand.

scious. With any of us, some of these zones may be fertile and evenly formed, others depleted, and others even treacherous. Some may be too arid, and others too humid. Some may be in a state of change from one condition to another; others may have stayed as they are for eons.

The major and minor lines of the hands are comparable to roadways—paths along which thought energy can course. Every line traverses a section of the palm with an origin and termination on specific mounts. The line's quality, effectiveness, and the smoothness of the journey upon it are influenced by the nature of the land upon which it has been carved. A line that travels across well-developed mounts will yield better results than one that traverses negatively developed ones.

In order to be able to interpret the lines—and their effects on your relationships—it is essential to have an understanding of the underlying mounts.

The following case illustrates how important the mounts are in influencing the effects of the lines.

Margo: Triumph over All Obstacles

Within a period of one year, Margot, recently divorced and living alone with her daughter, confronted several major challenges. Her mother, to whom she was very close, died after painful months of battling cancer; shortly after, her daughter decided to leave home. Both events forced her to redefine her sense of identity. Then her best friend was diagnosed with a terminal illness and given only a few months to live. In addition, she was under some pressure at work to accept a promotion she didn't really want. The emotional shock is registered in her Mars positive in the left print. That she survived and became stronger as a result of her experiences is confirmed by the radical development of her Mars in the right print as well as a longer head line.

An indented or deflated Mars positive indicates a feeling of being overwhelmed. Yet at these times, one can make the choice to give in to the exhaustion or to call upon resources of energy and will within. You can use inner strength to overcome obstacles that may appear insurmountable. This is the property of Mars positive. In Margot's case, the underlying mount of Mars positive became stronger as a result of

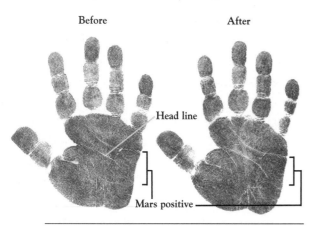

Before   After

Head line

Mars positive

Margot's experiences made her stronger, as seen in the development of her Mars and the longer head line.

her determination and will to confront these challenging situations. Just as a bridge is only as strong as its underlying supports, so the strengthened mount of Mars positive allowed her head line to grow deeper and longer. Margot felt she had no choice but to deal with the events in her life one day at a time. The longer head line indicates her perseverance and her ultimate triumph.

Your Superconscious: The Mounts

The hand is divided into segments called mounts. Each mount relates to a corresponding planet with a specific portfolio. The mounts of the hand provide a tangible record of how you deal with each of these planetary influences, and what your challenges are.

The mounts also represent the colors in the spectrum of the rainbow. The more each mount begins to reflect the characteristics of its own specific light frequency, the more representative it becomes of the superconscious soul, or light, within.

The mounts are Luna, Venus, Mars (formed by its negative and positive poles), Jupiter, Saturn, Sun, Mercury, Rahu, and Ketu.

The mount of Luna (or Moon) represents the first stage of the evolutionary process. Luna stands for the original plan of creation, as in the Bible quotation, "in the beginning was the Word." As such, it relates to the collective unconscious as well as to each person's individual receptivity to tune in to that creative source. Luna pertains to the qualities of perception, creativity, imagination, and sensory awareness.

Venus, next in the sequence of mounts, represents the actual physical manifestation of the "concept" that was initiated in Luna. ("And the

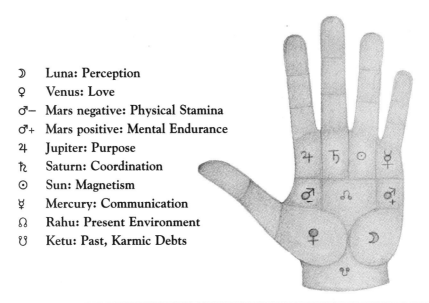

☽   Luna: Perception
♀   Venus: Love
♂–   Mars negative: Physical Stamina
♂+   Mars positive: Mental Endurance
♃   Jupiter: Purpose
♄   Saturn: Coordination
☉   Sun: Magnetism
☿   Mercury: Communication
☊   Rahu: Present Environment
☋   Ketu: Past, Karmic Debts

Your superconscious: the mounts.

Word was made flesh."*) Venus represents the actual cellular makeup—or energy—that manifests itself in physical form. It shows the condition of the body and how at home you feel in your physical form. The mount of Venus reflects the presence or absence of qualities such as harmony, kindness, grace, charm, and love. It reflects your degree of physical and sexual health, sensuality, and sense of beauty.

Mars negative is the next focus of attention for the unfolding human soul. Symbolically, it relates to the mobilization of the spark of incarnate energy originally conceived and then brought into being through Luna and then Venus. Mars negative stands for your energy, which, when not properly harnessed and channeled, can lead to exhaustion, or possibly to anger and aggression.

Jupiter represents the awakening of the con-

scious mind. In India, it is referred to as the guru, or dispeller of darkness. It speaks of your sense of purpose—what role you want to play in life. Jupiter stands for ambition, confidence, leadership, and justice.

Saturn indicates the necessity to search within. It represents the alchemist who is able to synthesize the experiences of Jupiter to extract a deeper meaning of life. Saturn stands for wisdom and discernment.

The Sun in the hand indicates our desire to share all that has been learned from the profound nature of Saturn. It represents the soul. The Sun shows that aspect within you that can transcend any limitations. Success, charisma, and integrity are all characteristics of the Sun.

In India, Mercury stands for the Buddha and reflects an enlightened consciousness. It relates to your involvement in the world, and also to your ability to detach from the fruits of your actions. Mercury denotes intuition, spontaneity,

*Book of John, Chapter 1, verse 14.

and the ability to communicate effortlessly.

Next lies the mount of Mars positive (which, with Mars negative—located on the opposite side of the palm—forms the Mars galaxy). As Mars negative relates to physical energy, Mars positive deals with mental strength. Positive characteristics include endurance, persistence, and a calm mental state.

Rahu and Ketu are inextricably intertwined. Ketu represents the kinds of circumstances attracted in the past and your attitudes toward them, whereas Rahu relates to the immediate environment. A famous Sanskrit verse tells us that "our present is the result of all our yesterdays, and the future depends on how well we live today." This sums up the relationship between Rahu and Ketu.

Ketu is your karmic account book, whose balance sheet portrays the entire record of your thoughts, attitudes, and behavior of the past. Rahu reflects the kind of environment you are likely to attract in the present, and how receptive you are to either making the most of it or limiting its potential by resisting opportunities.

From a metaphysical viewpoint, as the mounts begin to express the ideal characteristics for which they stand—for example, the objective perception of Luna, the unconditional love of Venus, the calmly active energy of Mars—they consequently begin to radiate at their specific light frequencies in the color spectrum. The result is pure radiant light.

Your Subconscious: The Major Lines

The sages of India have classified the lines into two groups—major and minor. The subconscious mind is shown by the three principal, or major, lines of heart, head, and life that indicate how we feel, think, and live, respectively. The minor lines—which include the line of destiny, the Sun line, and union line, among others—reflect the workings of the conscious mind.

From the formation of the major lines you can detect positive and negative patterns of thought as well as the likelihood of breaking old unconscious habits and the possibilities of formulating new positive ones. Through understanding the laws of cause and effect, you can see how receptive you are to learning from the past and recognizing that you are the creator of your own suffering and happiness.

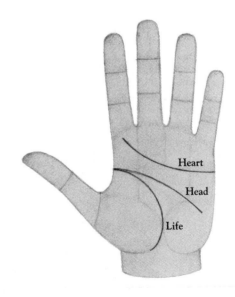

Your subconscious: the major lines. Heart line: how you love. *Head line:* how you think. *Life line:* how you live.

In Sanskrit the three major (subconscious) lines are referred to as *hradaya rekha* (heart line), *mastak rekha* (head line), and *jeevan rekha* (life line). They play a vital function, providing an interface between the superconscious mounts that underlie them and the conscious-related minor lines that give them expression.

BRIEF DIAGNOSTIC
SCOPE OF THE LIFE LINE

An analysis of the life line yields valuable information about your physical well-being. The line's formation indicates the state of health, the degree of stamina, and the condition of the nervous system. It also reveals the extent of your enthusiasm for life, and your willingness to undertake challenges.

From a spiritual viewpoint, the life line indicates your degree of self-control and ability to concentrate and focus. The life line can also be studied for clues to life events that chronicle the major influences affecting lifestyle, such as family influences, health obstacles, and interpersonal conflicts.

BRIEF DIAGNOSTIC
SCOPE OF THE HEAD LINE

The head line relates directly to the intellectual faculties of an individual. From a physical standpoint, it yields information regarding the actual organic condition of the brain.

Psychologically, this line reflects your degree of intelligence, mental refinement, and concentration. In addition, the potential for such spiritual qualities as intuition, composure, and dedication are seen here. Specific life events also register on the head line, particularly those that affect your mental health, psychological outlook, and ability to perceive objectively.

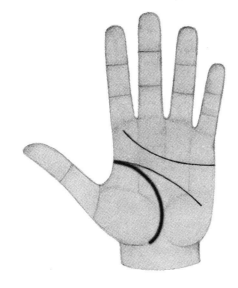

The life line.

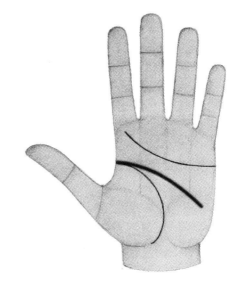

The head line.

BRIEF DIAGNOSTIC
SCOPE OF THE HEART LINE

The heart line serves as an indicator of your loving disposition, emotional makeup, and sexual well-being; it also provides information concerning the physical condition of the heart organ itself. From a spiritual standpoint, the heart line bears an especially close relationship to the soul, reflecting as it does the capacity for engendering the qualities of generosity and forgiveness. Chronological life events also register on this major line—most particularly, events relating to interpersonal relationships and emotional complexities.

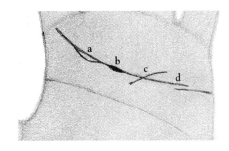

Negative markings on the heart line: (a) island, (b) dot, (c) interference line, and (d) overlapping lines.

pression, each of these lines should be deep, narrow, relatively long, and preferably free from any breaks or interferences.

In the presence of islands, dots, interference lines, overlapping lines, or any other negative signs, there is a necessity to take proper precautions in the area denoted by the line on which these negative markings appear.

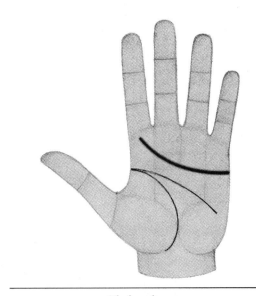

The heart line.

INTERPLAY OF THE THREE MAJOR LINES

When viewed together, these three major lines give you a clear understanding of how well you are utilizing and coordinating physical, mental, and emotional energies with your personality, experience, and behavior. For the healthiest ex-

Your Conscious: The Minor Lines

The minor (conscious) lines show to what extent you have been able to dive into your subconscious in order to bring its wealth to the surface of consciousness.

The minor lines signal an awakening. They appear on the hand as we become motivated to experience life more consciously. Once a person experiences the revelation of consciousness, living mechanically is no longer satisfying; you are compelled to move forward and discover deeper truths.

Following is a brief explanation of three of the most important minor lines: the destiny, Sun, and Mercury lines. Other minor lines that have a direct influence on relationships will be discussed later.

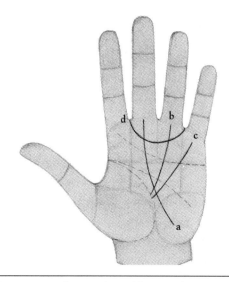

Your conscious: the minor lines. (a) Destiny line: vocation.
(b) Sun line: success. (c) Mercury line: communication.
(d) Girdle of Venus: creativity.

DESTINY LINE

The destiny line serves as the backbone for the other lines of the hand. It indicates the degree of your desire to structure your life. As a conscious line, it provides the outlet for the major lines of heart, head, and life to express themselves. A destiny line indicates that you have something to live for, to be in love with, and to be dedicated to, and that you have the motivation and focus to achieve your life ambition. The destiny line serves as a medium through which previously untapped qualities can be brought to a conscious level of expression by way of a profession or vocation.

The destiny line reveals the extent to which you are anchored in your own unique purpose. Finding your purpose, you are better prepared to enter into a relationship based on the fundamental strength of your own character.

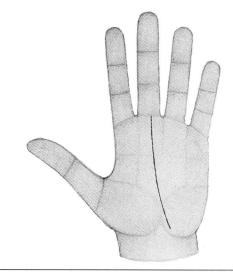

Destiny line.

SUN LINE

While the destiny line reflects your efforts, the Sun line speaks of the successful fruition of your work. The Sun line develops as a result of your belief and satisfaction in what you are doing. The aura of magnetism that you create around yourself subsequently attracts the appropriate circumstances and associates into your life.

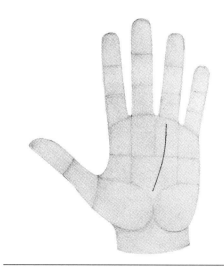

Sun line.

MERCURY LINE

The formation of a strong Mercury line in the hand indicates that an effortless ability to communicate with others has been developed.

When the Mercury line is fragmented, it indicates that you are not satisfied with your circumstances and surroundings. If such distress is not resolved, a variety of health problems can ensue, leading to the miscommunication that lies at the base of much of the unhappiness in relationships; these can be of an emotional, mental, physical, or sexual nature.

(A)

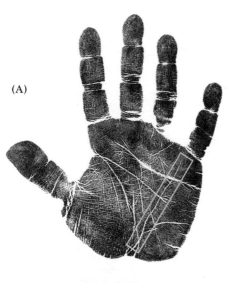

(B)

(A) Strong and (B) fragmented Mercury line.

The Importance of Creating a Balance between the Major and Minor Lines

The presence of major lines without the support of minor lines suggests a life lived unreflectively; either you are not aware of your rich inner potential, or you have not learned how to focus your unique passion and bring it into being. The presence of too many minor lines prevents one from accessing the subconscious; you are so overwhelmed with day-to-day detail that you have no time for reflection. It is best when the major lines are equal in strength to the minor lines. This allows the potential resources of the subconscious to find a conscious outlet of expression.

The following story of Houdini illustrates the circumstances that can occur when the major and minor lines are imbalanced. While Houdini was performing one of his great escape routines, he was bound inside a chest that was lowered through a hole in the ice. He had not calculated the strength of the current and so the chest, along with Houdini, was carried some distance downstream. When he escaped from the trunk and swam to the surface he could not find the hole to exit.

It is essential for the subconscious mind to find an outlet. If the minor lines are not present, or too weakly defined, one runs the risk of trapping one's potential within the subconscious. It was necessary for Houdini to find his outlet—the hole in the ice—to escape unharmed.

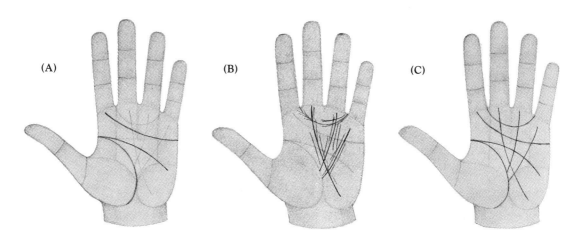

Balance between the major and minor lines. (A) Strong major lines, faint minor lines, (B) too many minor lines, (C) major lines equal to minor lines.

THREE CASE HISTORIES

Gary: Absence of Minor Lines

Gary had just gone through a divorce that left him physically and emotionally drained at the time of the first print. He understood that part of the reason for his failed relationship was his inability to express himself freely and openly. Many ideas and goals were subdued due to his lack of confidence. This frustration can be seen in his hand by the absence of minor lines (see

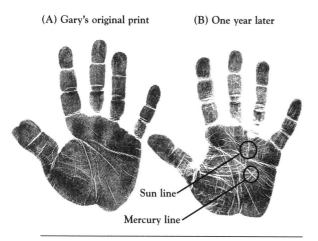

(A) Gary's original print   **(B) One year later**

Sun line

Mercury line

Immense changes that have taken place in the period of one year.

print A, below). For example, there is no Mercury line (which relates to self-expression) or Sun line (relating to belief in oneself). Gary decided to leave the past anguish and heartache behind and to focus on the future. He began group therapy, returned to school, and tried to maintain a positive outlook on life. The later print shows the development of both a Mercury line and a Sun line, revealing greater ease of self-expression and inner contentment.

Mick: Too Many Minor Lines

This individual was the manager of a busy food-store chain. On the verge of burnout, Mick realized that he had to regain control of his life. The excess of minor lines reflects his agitated state of mind (see print A, p. 18). He began yoga classes and breathing exercises, which we can see reflected in an improvement in the balance between the major and minor lines in the later print (see print B, p. 18). Mick is now back at the same job. However, due to his change in attitude, he is now able to cope with the same level of stress.

Too many conscious lines can result when you are preoccupied with the demanding environment around you. An overabundance of minor lines is like having a garden overrun with weeds. You need to prune the excessive minor lines in order for the subconscious to express itself more easily.

 **(A) Mick's original print**   **(B) Six months later**

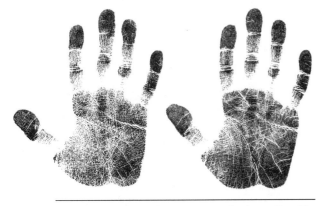

Finding inner calm results in minimizing the chaos reflected by an overabundance of conscious (minor) lines.

Pierre: Major and Minor Lines Equal

Pierre is a chiropractor who loves his work. He is confident and self-assured and highly regarded by his family, friends, and many clients. Pierre's minor lines of destiny, Mercury, and Sun are as equally developed as the three major lines of heart, head, and life. When the major and minor lines are equal, you can access your deepest level of awareness, your superconscious. In Pierre's case, this connection manifests as an ability to heal. Being attuned to this unlimited source of energy, he has become an open channel—a person who can receive and transmit healing vibrations.

The balance between Pierre's major and minor lines reflects confidence and passion for living that comes from recognizing his abilities and weaving them into the fabric of his life.

INTERPLAY BETWEEN LINES AND MOUNTS

The degree to which you find a balance between the mounts, the major lines, and the minor lines indicates to what extent you have integrated your superconscious, subconscious, and conscious minds.

WHICH HAND SHOULD YOU CONSULT?

Both hands should be studied for you to understand more about your thoughts and habits of the past and how they influence your will to change in the present. Both hands combined portray the struggles that you experience in working to overcome self-imposed limitations. In comparing both hands, you can gain an understanding of where you are coming from and where you are headed.

Determining the Active Hand

As soon as your brain–hand coordination is established in infancy, there is a natural inclination toward using one side of the body more than the other. The spontaneous inclination to use one hand over the other for such dexterous applications as writing or using tools reveals the dominant hand. In palmistry, the dominant hand—be it the right or the left—is known as the active hand. Ninety-nine percent of the time, the active hand will show a more progressive pattern of lines and signs than the less dominant hand. This reflects an evolution of consciousness taking place from old thought and behavior patterns toward a resolve for positive change in the future.

In rare cases, a person may not be using the more progressive hand (in terms of more positive lines and signs) as the dominant one. An Eastern perspective views this phenomenon as the person's inability or extreme reluctance to embrace life. He or she holds back rather than fully utilizing his or her potential.

Once the active hand has been determined, a true picture of the progressive pattern of thinking can be seen. The inactive hand shows the entirety of the prenatal experiences (see box), which have resulted in specific patterns of behavior. The inactive hand indicates ingrained

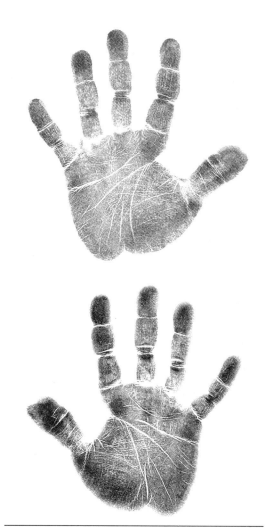

The study of both hands reveals how thoughts and habits from your past form the template that determines present behavior, unless you make a conscious effort to change. Note the development of the heart line in the (top) active hand (present) compared to the (bottom) inactive hand (past).

WHAT DO WE MEAN BY THE PAST?

The ancient texts of *Samudrik Shastra* state that the past includes the three most recent lifetimes. Time is relative. Whether it took a day, a month, a year, or an entire lifetime to form a habit, the inactive hand contains the sum total of all those traits that have resulted in who we are today. These include inherited genetic traits that may skip a few generations, but show up again in the makeup of a grandchild sometime in the future.

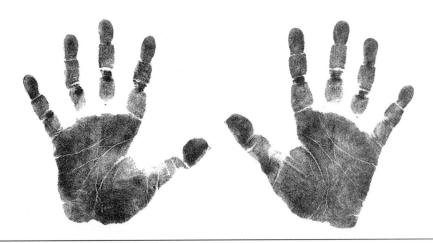

The progressive pattern of Sylvia's heart line in the active right hand shows her desire to be more expressive.
(Left) inactive, past; (right) active, present.

habits from the past. How these habits will influence the present and future is seen by weighing the strength of the inherited traits together with the progressive influences seen in the active hand. Depending on whether past habits are positive or negative, they will either help or hinder your evolution.

After understanding the importance and significance of checking both hands to see your evolutionary progress—specifically with regard to the quality of your relationships—now take a look at the heart line.

A comparative analysis of the heart line as seen in both hands reveals the evolutionary process unfolding in the emotional makeup of the individual. Ideally, the heart line should be making progress from the inactive to the active hand.

In the case of the hands shown on page 19, the individual is left-handed. Consequently the left hand is reflecting the present circumstances and the right hand is inactive, showing the habits of the past. To understand the progress taking place we must see the inactive hand in relation to the active hand. We find an improve-

ment in the heart line confirmed by the length and rounder formation.

Sylvia: Expansive Heart

As a child Sylvia used to recite multiplication tables in her head as soon as anyone aside from a family member came close to her. Painfully afraid of risking rejection, she distanced herself emotionally by holding her breath and counting. Fainting was often her release for pent-up emotion. As she grew older, her inhibition lessened as she gradually became more accustomed to relating with others. That she felt compelled to change is confirmed by the development of her heart line in the active, right hand.

The inactive hand reflects the habits you have already created for yourself. It is one thing to want to be more generous and open with your feelings, but without constantly substituting positive new actions for the old habits, you can easily fall back into old patterns.

Hand prints taken at regular intervals can confirm the progress a person makes. If the heart line in the active hand shrinks and begins to

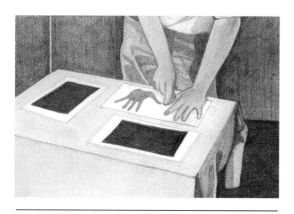

Taking hand prints.

resemble the heart line of the inactive hand, then the person is lacking either the supportive environment or the willpower to break new ground. If the inactive heart line grows to match the longer heart line of the active hand, that shows the desire to change is becoming a reality.

HEART LINE: BAROMETER OF YOUR LOVING DISPOSITION

The heart line plays a tremendous role in showing you whom you are likely to attract; it also reveals your capacity to feel deeply for them.

Once you are able to decipher the code embedded in your heart line, you will learn much about your capacity to love. By consciously applying yourself to growing and refining this line, you can alter your personal magnetism and, consequently, improve the interpersonal relationships in your life.

What Do We Mean by Personal Magnetism?

We all know people who, when they converse, hold their listeners spellbound. Others command attention simply by walking into a room. Saints and tyrants, rock stars and political leaders: what power allows these people to exercise such influence over others?

Just as iron filings are attracted to the poles of a magnet, the personality of a spiritually strong person generates a personal magnetic field that has the power to draw others to him or her. In *The Divine Romance* Paramahansa Yogananda defines spiritual magnetism as "the power of the soul to attract or create whatever it needs for all-round happiness and well-being." The quality of your personal magnetism is linked to the state of your spiritual evolution. One way of developing personal magnetism is to cultivate the ability to love others unselfishly. When you express selfless love—for your family, your friends, your neighbors, your community—you become attractive to others. You become a magnetic person.

Daniel: Developing Personal Magnetism

Daniel, a childcare worker, wanted to get along better with his friends and colleagues. He was encouraged to develop his heart line, which at the time of the first print was faint. He persisted each day, visualizing his heart line growing. He tried daily to incorporate all the ideal qualities that a longer heart line reflects; for example, he practiced expressing empathy and concern for how others were feeling. Within three months, he found himself more approachable as people began to relate to him more easily. By allowing his heart to open, he

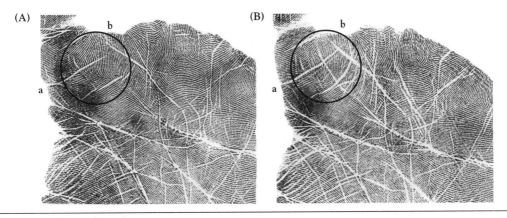

Daniel's active right hand: (A) Original print and (B) eighteen months later.
In the encircled areas, note that the later print shows that the heart line has grown.

increased his magnetism, which can be seen in the expansion of the heart line.

In the encircled areas of both prints (shown above), note how the heart line has grown an extension toward the Jupiter finger. Also, note the development of the Ring of Solomon on the mount of Jupiter (a–b). This sign of wisdom reflects an ability to understand the psychology of people. It is found on the hands of many individuals in the helping professions.

Attracting Meaningful Relationships: Cause and Effect

In this world of duality, attracting a meaningful relationship is not a simple thing. Most people think that a relationship with someone is the cause that creates the effect of happiness in life. In fact, this is not so. In essence, your magnetic range is primarily the cause and the person you attract is simply the effect.

If you are dissatisfied with your relationships, then isn't it logical to start investigating the cause in order to create a better effect? If you can enhance and strengthen your personal magnet-

ism, you can improve the interpersonal relationships in your life.

What Is Happiness?

When you ask yourself where happiness has gone, you should really be asking yourself just what happiness is. In Hindu texts, happiness is referred to as a combination of three things: *sat, chit,* and *ananda. Sat* means permeated with absolute truth. *Chit* is an intuitive feeling in the heart, completely unclouded by selfishness, anger, or fear. *Ananda* means joy saturated with bliss. Happiness then is a calm, collected, and harmonious feeling beyond cause and effect. It is transcendent in its nature—pure, nourishing, and unconditional.

What Will Happen When I Look for the Cause in Myself?

When you experience hurt in your personal relationships, you have a natural tendency to blame others for your pain. You often situate the prob-

The god Krishna with his beloved Radha.

lem outside of yourself; you may even become preoccupied with your partner and hold him or her responsible for your unhappiness. However, harboring such thoughts only makes you feel more frustrated, angry, or withdrawn.

Now you are being asked to concentrate on developing a better heart line. Won't that make you feel even more vulnerable? Wouldn't it be better to just find a new relationship or a more perfect partner?

We often put our hope in the belief that the ideal partner will suddenly materialize as the answer to all our problems. Or we sometimes find ourselves involved with someone who is not really free or available. If you are not happy, you have to ask yourself why you didn't establish very clear criteria for yourself and your partner. Or, if you did establish such criteria then you must wonder why you have compromised.

The fact of the matter is that often we are not specific enough in our priorities. We can mislead ourselves into thinking that we have learned from our mistakes. But have we really? And if so, why do we keep on repeating the same mistakes?

Emotions often play hide and seek. As you begin to accept responsibility for the events in your life, you come to realize that perhaps you have never really taken an honest look at why you want to attract someone in the first place. You may have been more preoccupied with your own desire to meet the right person rather than developing those qualities that would naturally draw that person to you.

Creating a better cause in yourself by increasing your self-awareness can lead toward the effect of greater personal magnetism and happiness. But along the way many new thoughts and questions may arise: "Will I be able to withstand the pressure once I begin taking responsibility for my own thoughts and actions?" "Will I be able to keep my heart open in the face of other people's unpredictable behavior?"

The answer is, yes. Initially, those around you may react with surprise when you no longer respond with your usual reactive habits, and instead, are open to discussion based on genuine listening and freedom of expression. By remaining calm and loving, you can diffuse potentially disruptive situations. By turning the blinds of your introspective window differently, you begin to see people in a new light, no longer simply taking them at face value. Objective self-analysis is the key to realizing differences and making the appropriate changes in attitudes toward others.

Often two people are drawn together by mutual desire. However, desire alone cannot form the basis of a deep and loving relationship. A lifelong bond depends on mutual commitment wherein both partners nourish the other in the quest for self-knowledge. Mutual "usefulness" is at the heart of a lasting, loving relationship. However, you need to be able to discriminate between what you want (or think you want) and what you need. For example, you can be attracted to somebody for reasons of "chemistry," and mistake desire for love. The person you really need to be with, however, may not be so obviously attractive, but may have the deeper qualities that complement yours. If you choose wisely, the partner you need will be the one you deeply love—and want—for your entire life.

Now the question arises, "How can I build successful relationships?" It is a complex question to answer. Let us try to understand this puzzle in the light of the heart line and its relationship to the other lines and signs in the hand.

2
The Heart Line: Your Emotional Gauge

The Sanskrit term for heart line is *hradaya rekha*. One translation of the root *hra* is the potential to give and the capacity to receive. The words embody the concept that the dynamic process of achieving successful human relationships is reflected in the heart line. The heart line functions smoothly when there is a spontaneous and continuous cycle of giving and receiving, no matter what level we are functioning on: physical, sexual, emotional, psychological, or spiritual.

SCOPE OF THE HEART LINE

Let us begin with a brief overview of the significance of the heart line in daily life. On a physical level, the heart line indicates the actual organic strength of the heart. In a psychological sense, the heart line gives information about temperament as shown through feelings, moods, and responses. Emotional and sexual stability and behavior, as well as the degree of indulgence in these areas, is also evident.

On a spiritual level, this line indicates the potential to sacrifice for a need greater than one's own. Additionally, qualities associated with expanded self-awareness, such as sincerity, generosity, joy, compassion, and forgiveness, are also indicated. The heart line shows the potential for conjugal as well as divine love.

Various irregularities in the heart line, indicating a break in the natural flow of the give-and-take cycle, signal problems. Emotional vulnerability, lack of self-control, emotional losses, disappointment—and the consequent stress on the heart—all register on this major line. The heart line also indicates the degree to which you can absorb emotionally shocking experiences and your capacity to recover from them. Further, the timing of significant events can be deduced from the heart line, including major and minor emotional influences—both positive and negative—and the types of situations and people that you may attract at different times in your life.

The heart line reflects your potential to develop successful human relationships. Once you know how to read the heart line and interpret the information that it contains, you can use it to assess your emotional well-being. The following information is a practical guide to understanding your feelings through the study of the heart line.

ple, a divorce at the age of thirty-five—the heart line is not, in fact, predicting the occurrence. Such a feature on the heart line may be a sign that unless we recognize the potential for marital difficulty and take steps toward resolving problems with our partner, the marriage may end—an unfortunate outcome. However, it could equally point to inherent problems that cannot be resolved regarding choice of partner; divorce may be a positive step—a welcome release from an unsuitable match. The event in itself, then, is neither certain nor necessarily negative.

The concept of time is a complex one. We speak about past, present, and future; however, we also recognize the artificiality of these terms: tomorrow becomes today in a matter of hours, and yesterday exists only as a memory. You can resolve this apparent ambiguity if you recognize that what you think of as the passing of time is actually the dynamic process of continually incorporating the implications of past acts, and dreams (or fears) for the future, into your

JOURNEY OF THE HEART LINE

You find the heart line traveling across the hand from its origin on the mount of Jupiter, past Saturn and Sun, and terminating on the mount of Mercury. Roughly speaking, this line passes through four time "zones": childhood, (age 0–21), youth (21–42), middle age (42–63) and old age (63 on). Certain features found on the heart line point to specific events in our lives. These events may be actual occurrences, such as a birth, marriage, or death; they may also be less tangible—periods of emotional well-being or distress, or even strong tendencies toward a particular behavior. Even though these events are related to a seemingly particular time—for exam-

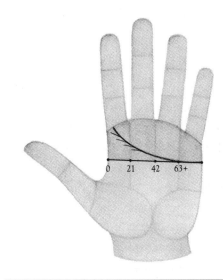

The journey of the heart line across the four time zones of the palm.

conscious awareness of the present. You can do nothing to change what happened in the past, but you can choose how it affects you and how you are going to deal with it. For example, a young man who had an abusive father can perpetuate the cycle of abuse, or he can seek help to become compassionate and loving in his own relationships. We cannot dictate future happenings, but we can work at developing tendencies that may lead to positive outcomes and minimizing tendencies that may lead to negative outcomes. The more you learn to grow in the present the more effectively you can reshape your conscious awareness of both the past and the future. Such deeper self-knowledge changes the architecture of the lines of the hand.

Linked to this notion of time is karma, the principle that past actions have consequences in the present and, by extension, in the future. Whatever you do changes the present and sets in motion a chain reaction of events. If you have been so self-absorbed that you have not developed a sensitivity to the needs of those around you, you may find there is no one reaching out to support you when you need help. Isolation is a direct result of neglecting to build deep friendships. If you develop an attitude of caring and compassion for others, you are often surprised by unexpected displays of generosity. For example, a young teacher, well-known for her kindness and understanding toward students, returned home one night to find her house burned to the ground. The following morning, her friends and colleagues came to her rescue with food, clothing, and furniture. The generosity she experienced was a direct result of her own unselfish nature.

In order to divide the heart line into the four time zones, it is important to locate and divide the four mounts of Jupiter, Saturn, Sun, and Mercury. The borders forming each mount signify ends and beginnings of major life cycles.

How to Locate the Four Time Zones

Find point A (where the Jupiter finger meets the palm) and point B (where the thumb meets the palm). Imagine a line (AB) between points A and B and bisect it at point C. Find point D (where the Mercury finger meets the palm) and extend D to E equal to AC. Connect CE. This is the base line of the mental mounts. Bisect line CE at F; CF at G; and FE at H. Draw perpendicular lines GI, FJ, and HK. These form the mounts of Jupiter, Saturn, Sun, and Mercury. The time zones CG, GF, FH, and HE cover the years 0–21, 21–42, 42–63, and 63 on, respectively.

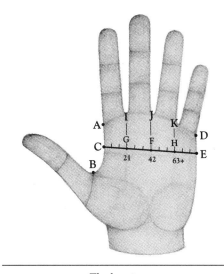

The four time zones.

Each of these sections is further subdivided into three segments of seven years each.

What Is the Significance of Heart-Line Placement?

None of the lines of the hand can be seen in isolation. We find the heart line in the realm of sattwa, traveling across the mounts of Jupiter, Saturn, Sun, and Mercury.

The fact that the heart line is located in sattwa and not tamas or rajas is significant. Tamas is home of the life line, which is concerned mainly with breathing, sleeping, eating, and procreating. The head line is located in rajas, where the mind is confronted with the realities of survival. Due to its location in the sattwic area of the palm, the heart line is well-suited to expressing the ideal qualities of unconditional love because it is free from the concerns of physical or material survival.

It would be an oversimplification, however, to suggest that all life lines are tamasic, and that

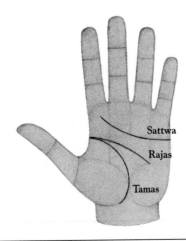

The three major lines of heart, head, and life are located in their respective areas of sattwa, rajas, *and* tamas.

all heart lines are sattwic. In fact, as we begin to examine different heart-line examples, it will become clear that some are visibly rajasic, some more tamasic, others more sattwic—or, more typically a combination of the above. The heart line, therefore, is not immune to the physical preoccupations of tamas, nor to the rajasic impulse for material survival.

MOUNTS

The lines of the hand are governed by the nature of the mounts that lie beneath them. The life line is ideally situated encircling the areas of Venus and Mars negative. These two mounts represent the body and its capacity to be animate. The life line serves as a channel through which *prana*, the life force, can breathe life into the body.

The head line reflects powers of logic and deduction and our intellectual ability to make rational decisions. Navigating through the rajasic world of the Mars galaxy, it draws the energy of Mars to put decisions into action.

The heart line travels across the sattwic area of the palm. The lofty and humanitarian nature of the mounts of Jupiter, Saturn, Sun, and Mercury provides the environment in which unconditional love can grow.

It is a universal principle that the observable world, the subliminal and the transcendent, are interconnected. Saint Teresa of Avila said that we must never be out of touch with the underground stream (the soul) within us. The yogis of India tell us we are nourished by prana. The Bible says we do not live by bread alone. The Chinese refer to this life force within as chi.

The physical body is subject to the laws of

Mars negative ♂−
Mars positive ♂+
Venus ♀
Jupiter ♃
Saturn ♄
Sun ☉
Mercury ☿
Rahu ☊

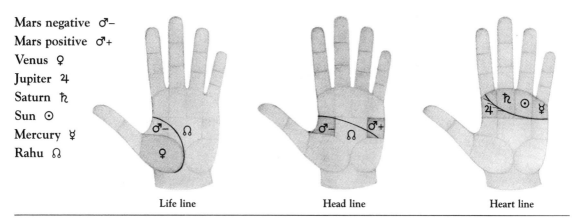

Life line   Head line   Heart line

Each of the major lines is governed by the nature of the mounts that lie beneath them.

gravity, time, and space. Compared to the causal (superconscious or transcendent) and astral (subconscious or subliminal) forms, it is the densest form of consciousness. In palmistry, horizontal lines signify struggle. Gravity, as well as other physical constraints, takes hold. The horizontal lines portray this downward-pulling force, unlike the vertical ones, which show ease of transcendence. The heart line, then, registers the incarnation of the soul. The horizontal passage of the heart as it journeys across the sattwic realm of the palm signifies the individual's struggle to rediscover the superconscious, or soul, within. We have a choice: we can view this struggle negatively, as a source of personal restriction and confinement, or we can transform the pain of struggle into an opportunity for growth. The heart line is a personal record of how you handle this struggle.

The Quadrangle: Landing Strip of the Angels

In order to interpret the heart line, you need to examine it in relation to the head line. Together

they create an area known as the quadrangle (a four-sided shape with opposite sides of equal length), sometimes called the "landing strip of the angels." These lines are inseparable and represent the two sides of your nature: the heart indicates your feeling or positive (+) pole, and the head, your reason or negative (−) pole. The length of the lines, the distance between the lines, their position and their formation on the hand all determine the extent to which the quadrangle is balanced.

The two lines of heart and head should be equal in length and should not touch, as any joining or overlapping creates a short circuit similar to that in electricity. Ideally, these lines should have a slight tendency toward an hourglass shape with the distance between them neither too narrow nor too wide. Lastly, given that the heart and head lines are balanced with each other, the quadrangle should be positioned neither too high in the hand nor too low.

It takes effort to develop a balance between these two aspects. For example, if the head line overpowers the heart line, you may rationalize your feelings. If the heart line overpowers the head line, you may be emotionally biased when you make decisions. When you achieve a balance between your reason and feeling, neither one pulls the other out of alignment. In the peace and serenity created through this equilibrium, you become receptive to "angel visits" in the form of good friends, wise teachers, visionary dreams, intuition, and sound advice.

Locating Heart Line and Head Line

The diagram serves to give a point of reference, enabling you to locate the lines of heart and head, which form the quadrangle.

Find point A (where the Jupiter finger meets the palm) and point B (where the thumb meets the palm). Find midpoint C on line AB. The heart line ideally originates near point A and the head line at point C. Next, find point D (where the Mercury finger meets the palm) and extend D to E equal to AC. Extend DE to point F (EF equal to DE). The heart line ideally ter-

minates at point E, and the head line near point F. Connect points AE (heart line) and CF (head line) in a gentle arc. These four points, AECF, outline the ideal quadrangle placement.

Effects of a Balanced Quadrangle

In Eastern metaphysics, there are two currents, called *pingla* and *ida*, that circulate in the spine: one is hot and the other cold. They are represented by the heart line and the head line respectively. When they come together, a third current in the spine, called the *sushumna*, is activated. A balanced quadrangle signifies the blending of these warm and cool currents that meet in the sushumna, creating a condition that, like Goldilocks's porridge, is "just right." On a physical level, this condition is experienced as a healthy body temperature of 37 degrees Celsius, which is felt as neither hot nor cold.

In the quadrangle, this neutral, balanced condition signifies a healthy spiritual state of being. It is shown by free-flowing energy between the heart and head, and emotional and physical ease. We feel free from distracting circumstances and are able to both think objectively and feel loving. Furthermore, within this calm interior environment, the ground is prepared for greater wisdom and receptivity.

A balanced quadrangle denotes reliability and maturity. There is a conscious awareness that life has a purpose, and that we have something useful to contribute to humanity. When passions overrule reason or logic subdues emotions, satisfying relationships are unlikely to flourish. Balance in the quadrangle indicates that you are ready for unconditional love: you

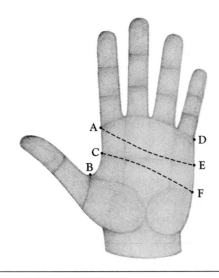

How to determine a balanced quadrangle.

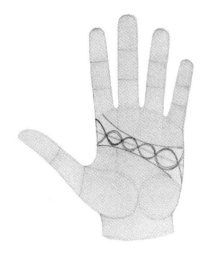

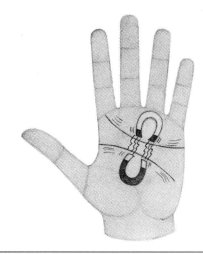

The heart and head lines create a magnetic field between them.

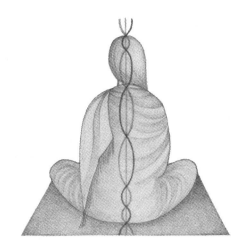

The heart and head lines, forming the quadrangle, reflect pingla (hot) and ida (cold) currents circulating in our spine.

are open to receiving love but do not demand it. When the mind is quiet and the heart is still you can enter into that sushumna state of inner peace. It is a state of loving—with yourself, with friends, with lovers, and with God.

IMPORTANCE OF THE DISTANCE BETWEEN HEART AND HEAD LINES

Whether in nature or spirit, everything in the universe is polarized. We define "day" in terms

of "not-day," which is "night." There is always a positive (+) pole, as characterized here by the heart line, and a negative (–) pole, the head line. A magnetic field becomes discernible when two magnets are slowly brought together. The strength of the field can be increased or decreased by narrowing or widening the gap between them.

BALANCED DISTANCE BETWEEN HEART AND HEAD LINES

The same electromagnetic dynamics found throughout the universe are also found in the hands. We are all human magnets. We attract or repel people and circumstances into and out of our lives.

This magnetic energy is found in the quadrangle. The distance between the heart and head lines determines the degree to which the quadrangle is balanced. A certain amount of tension—neither too much nor too little—between the head and heart is necessary to create synergy. The space created between the head and heart lines, wherein neither line pushes or

Balanced distance between the heart and head lines.

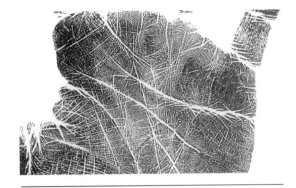

Narrow quadrangle.

pulls the other out of its natural placement, creates an ideal "landing strip for the angels."

NARROW QUADRANGLE

If you hold two magnets together without allowing them to touch, you feel tension. This is analogous to the tension that occurs in a narrow quadrangle. There is a feeling of constraint inside. You might feel tense, worried, or high-strung in dealing with people and situations. You may be unreceptive to correction and often temperamental. However, through meditation or relaxation techniques, you can learn to let go and relax.

It takes energy to deal with inner tension, which makes focusing beyond a narrow range of concerns difficult. There is a need for a broader, more flexible, outlook. It is important to make a conscious effort to create a positive environment that will allow a calm yet active temperament to grow.

WIDE QUADRANGLE

If magnets are held too far apart, little or no tension is felt. This is analogous to the lack of tension that occurs in a wide quadrangle. The head and heart lines appear to have lost touch with each other. They cannot resonate. Hence, a

wide quadrangle indicates a tendency to be out of touch. An appropriate degree of tension is necessary in order to deal with the conflicts of everyday life. If you avoid conflict, you become unconcerned and others may see you as aloof or flighty. A wide quadrangle may denote a lack of serious commitment; you may be somewhat careless in speech or actions.

A person subject to impetuous behavior often finds it difficult to concentrate long enough to make a connection with the sushumna. The "landing lights" of head and heart are so far apart that the landing strip itself is not apparent. You may not recognize the "angels" present in your environment that may

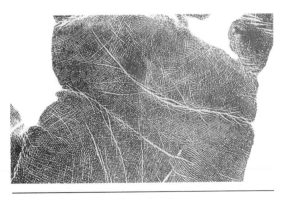

Wide quadrangle.

be manifested either as mentors and wise friends or as inner wisdom and intuition. Your relationships tend to be superficial or short-lived rather than profound and long-lasting.

It is important to be conscious of how your behavior affects those around you. If you are overly self-absorbed and isolated from others—possibly as a result of past hurt or disappointment—you may overlook the fact that others need you.

BOTTLENECK QUADRANGLE

Sometimes an otherwise balanced quadrangle may form a bottleneck where the heart and head lines are drawn toward each other. This formation reflects a tug-of-war between reason and feelings, creating uncertainty, especially at the time indicated by the narrowest section of the quadrangle. To help overcome these feelings of confusion, you need to cultivate a supportive environment.

Balanced origin with wide termination.

you may have become overly sensitive to the suffering that is natural to the human condition and respond to that by withdrawing from the pain of struggle. The lines grow farther apart as we distance ourselves from our environment. If you recognize this tendency, you can choose to accept each conflict as an opportunity for growth. Rather than becoming aloof, you can respond to each of life's challenges in a positive manner. A sensitive nature then becomes an asset rather than a liability. A healthy sense of humor can help you reestablish a proper connection between head and heart.

BALANCED ORIGIN, NARROW TERMINATION

This formation of the quadrangle indicates a tendency toward a high-strung emotional nature. The balanced origin denotes a receptivity to new ideas, surroundings, people, and relationships earlier in life. It shows sensitivity and a potential for joy and positive self-expression. However, the narrowing of the distance between the lines indicates that it may require more and more effort to be open to the environment. You may find yourself worrying about money, health,

Bottleneck.

BALANCED ORIGIN, WIDE TERMINATION

A balanced origin indicates a receptivity to new ideas and circumstances early in life. However,

Balanced origin with narrow termination.

being alone, not being alone, having too much, having too little—a whole host of concerns that eat into your energy and close you off from the joy of life. At the time when the quadrangle is at its narrowest, it is especially important to make a conscious effort to be relaxed, spontaneous, and affectionate.

NARROW ORIGIN, BALANCED TERMINATION

This formation indicates that relationships may begin with suspicion, doubt, and insecurity. It is indicative of a reluctance to trust others. There is a predisposition toward overcaution and self-protection. If you have this formation, you may find it difficult to let people into your heart or your confidence. Tension is created by too close a contact be-

tween mind and emotions. However, as time unfolds, you learn to open up and become more accepting. Freed from a worrying disposition, you find it increasingly easy to interact with people and encourage positive relationships.

NARROW ORIGIN, WIDE TERMINATION

The closed origin indicates a lack of trust. There is a constant need for intellectual clarification and proof of other people's love, which can inhibit the ability to respond to a loving environment.

There is a tendency toward suspicion, doubt, and hypersensitivity. If these feelings are not checked, you may be disposed to losing interest in relating with others and feel that no one really understands you. You worry that others may not fulfill your expectations of them, you are disappointed when they do not, and you withdraw from future encounters. Since other people rarely behave according to anyone's preconceptions, you can learn to enjoy being surprised if you are willing to abandon the cycle of expectation, disappointment, and withdrawal. In the later part of life, particularly, it is essential to maintain enthusiasm for people and life; otherwise, an attitude of indifference can lead you to quietly slip off by yourself—away from it all.

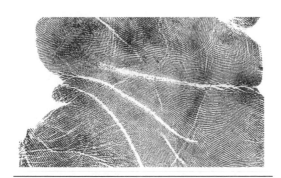

Narrow origin with balanced termination.

Narrow origin with wide termination.

WIDE ORIGIN, BALANCED TERMINATION

This formation shows a somewhat remote, passive attitude toward others and even toward the self. Although this character trait initially suggests a free spirit, there is a high price to pay in terms of building committed relationships. There is a lack of resonance between the intellect and emotions. You may see yourself as an independent being whose actions affect no one but yourself. The balanced termination, however, indicates a potential for developing greater focus and responsibility in life as well as in love.

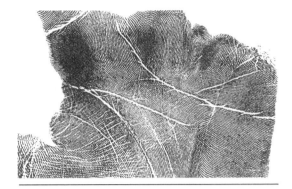

Wide origin with narrow termination.

Wide origin with balanced termination.

WIDE ORIGIN, NARROW TERMINATION

The wide origin characterizes the wish to be free-spirited, like Peter Pan. However, the desire to be carefree and independent is interpreted by others as a sign of irresponsibility and lack of involvement. The narrow termination suggests an attempt to become more involved with everyday matters even though an inappropriate degree of stress infuses your relationships.

Sometimes the heart line veers too near the head line. This indicates that, although you appear open and carefree, you may, in reality, be subconsciously controlling people and events. The mind may dominate the emotions, reducing situations to matters of simple logic. Sometimes the head line approaches too close to the heart line. In this case, your emotions disregard logic and you may direct situations through behavior that is irrational and emotionally subjective. In either scenario behavior is unpredictable.

If you have this configuration, and neither the origin nor the termination is in its proper placement, your perception may be biased. To regain a balanced viewpoint, you should practice relaxation techniques, which will allow you to open up to others.

Significance of Length of Heart and Head Lines

Whereas the distance between the lines signifies your desire, intention, and ability to form relationships, the length of the lines determines your staying power. To maintain a magnetic field, the poles must oppose each other; similarly, the head and heart lines must stand opposite throughout their length. The two equally

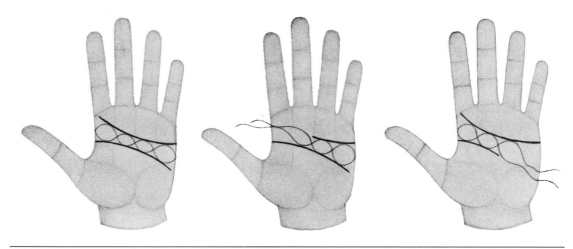

The balanced interweaving of emotions and reason (heart and head) unravels when the lines are of unequal length.

long lines sustain the appropriate tension between them that holds the intellect and emotions in perfect balance.

BALANCED QUADRANGLE: HEART LINE EQUAL IN LENGTH TO HEAD LINE

The heart and head lines are analogous to the borders of neighboring states. Between these borders lies a neutral zone, which acts as a buffer to protect the integrity of each. The borders extend equally to preserve this neutral territory; otherwise, one nation might infringe upon the other, disturbing the peace. Thus, heart and head lines of the same length indicate dependability, reliability, stability, and cooperation in all forms of relationships.

INCOMPLETE QUADRANGLE: LONG HEART LINE, SHORT HEAD LINE

A long heart line denotes a generous capacity for love—both giving and receiving. However, a short head line ending in the center of the palm (mount of Rahu) is lost in the preoccupations of everyday living. It is unable to support the heart

Heart line equal in length to head line.

Long heart line with short head line.

line in its pursuit of a steadfast and committed relationship. It indicates a short-sighted perception of reality as circumscribed by personal priorities rather than one that is far-sighted and visionary.

This kind of quadrangle shows an ambiguous nature. At times, you may be open, sensitive, and emotionally attuned—qualities indicated by a long heart line. At other times, you may display a brusque, matter-of-fact attitude as a result of the short head line's influence on the heart. You feel the need to be more loving, but the head line does not support this expression. As your emotions are censored by the mind, there is a tendency to intellectualize your sentiments. For example, instead of giving unconditionally—a nonrational choice—you may hold back to maintain your material status quo—a pragmatic decision. Without the mutual support of head and heart, intuition cannot flourish. Your loving nature can be curbed when the mind creates misunderstandings by coloring your attitudes and your sincere responses to others.

INCOMPLETE QUADRANGLE: SHORT HEART LINE, LONG HEAD LINE

A long head line indicates that the mind is receptive to exploring new ideas. However, the mind needs the intuition of the heart to evaluate new ideas and their validity in your life. The shorter heart line in this configuration shows that you tend to view life primarily through the lens of your logic. Whatever emotional sensitivity you have tends to be directed toward yourself and your own needs. In this formation, you may have an enormous intellectual capacity; however, without the balancing overview of the heart line, you may rationalize and justify your behavior. You need to take precautions not to be

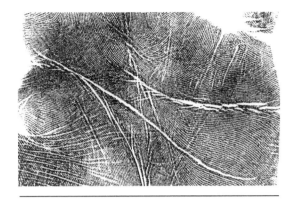

Short heart line with long head line.

so preoccupied with intellectual pursuits that you fail to develop loving, giving relationships.

Cycle of Breath Reflected in Quadrangle

Yogic tradition places great emphasis on the technique of breathing. Ideally, the incoming breath should be equal to the outgoing breath in depth and duration. This produces a balance

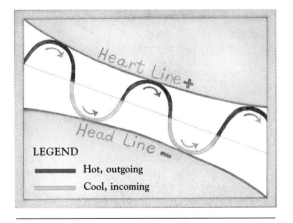

By learning to control your breathing so that you can achieve a balance between incoming and outgoing—cool and warm—currents, you can grow your head and heart lines equally, establishing a neutral zone.

between cool (incoming) and warm (outgoing) breathing that results in a neutral state. The life force—prana, or chi—can then flow without impediment.

Most of us recognize the benefit of taking a few deep breaths when we are anxious, stressed, or in pain. We are cooling down our overstimulated emotions; we are also giving our intellect an opportunity to distance us from the source of our unease. Similarly, we often sigh or exhale forcibly in response to sorrow, anger, or frustration. We are letting off steam, releasing an overabundance of heat; we are attempting to bring our feelings into balance with our intellect. In both instances there is an effort to reach a balance between emotions and reason—between heart and head.

When the heart and head lines are equal in length, you have a balanced quadrangle. Lines of unequal length indicate that either the heart or the head—the emotions or reason—is overpowering the other. In such cases of imbalance, the neutral state between hot and cold is unstable. You may have moments in your daily life when things are just right but you are unable to sustain this equilibrium. You may attract the wrong people, or the right people at the wrong time. By learning to control your breathing so that you can achieve a balance between incoming and outgoing—cool and warm—currents, you can grow your heart and head lines equally, establishing a neutral zone. You become centered in yourself as well as becoming synchronous with events and people around you. In this ideal state you are open to meeting and recognizing kindred spirits.

Significance of Position of Quadrangle

You can have the most fun flying a kite when it soars high in the sky while being firmly held. Similarly, a well-positioned quadrangle indicates that you are able to express your emotions freely without losing touch with reality.

The head line, which forms the base of the quadrangle, provides the junction between the sattwic and the tamasic worlds. The proper placement of the head line in the rajasic area of the palm indicates that you are centered in your being. A properly placed quadrangle shows that you are neither too philosophical nor too mundane. Just as a kite string allows the kite to soar heavenward while maintaining its link with Earth, your intellect (head line) allows your generous, idealistic, loving nature (heart line) to find expression in objective reality. When the quadrangle is displaced—in other words, when the lines of heart and head are too high or too low—you can be out of step with the people and events in your life. Sometimes you let go of your kite string and your fun is shortlived; sometimes you are unable to get your kite airborne, and all you have is frustration. If too idealistic, you are not able to temper your emotions with reason; if too rational, you lack inspiration.

WELL-PLACED HEART AND HEAD LINES

When the quadrangle formed by the lines of heart and head is well placed, you live in synchronicity with those around you. The proper placement of the heart and head lines allows you to view the affairs of your life from a calm, focused state of being. You are able to perceive the intentions of others and to act with common sense and intuitive understanding of oth-

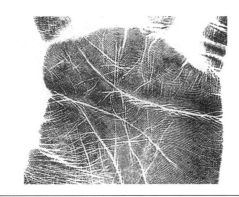

Well-placed heart and head lines.

ers' needs. Because you view the events of your life within the context of the world at large, you are able to feel empathy for others. You understand their pain and consequently can offer advice, love, and care without being judgmental. This placement of the quadrangle reflects the potential to attract healthy, happy, and harmonious relationships.

DISPLACED HEART AND HEAD LINES

Quadrangle Too Low

When the quadrangle is pulled down into the area of tamas, you may be unable to see beyond the immediate challenges and struggles that you encounter in life. You can become pessimistic or cynical as a result. You may find that establish-

ing harmonious relations can be difficult, as your limited, self-absorbed perspective tends to create a feeling of isolation. This placement can also affect your ability to make well-informed decisions. You should make a serious effort to be more receptive to the advice of friends and well-wishers.

Quadrangle Too High

When both lines are pulled up toward the world of sattwa, you tend to be overly enthusiastic and idealistic. Although you may have good intentions, you may act according to your own subjective, emotional impressions. In matters of love, you act on sentimental whims rather than out of a sensitivity to the genuine needs and desires of others. Consequently, it is difficult to build good relationships because you are disappointed by others' failures to live up to your expectations, which are often inappropriate. There is a danger of becoming arrogant, thinking that you are better than most people. Preconceived notions about how others should behave and interact with you—which are rarely shared—cause you to believe the world is a difficult place full of misunderstandings. However, it is hard for anyone to reach you when you are unhappy or absorbed in your own idealistic pursuits.

Quadrangle too low.

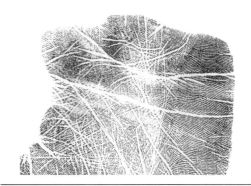

Quadrangle too high.

DISPLACED HEAD LINE PULLED TOWARD HEART LINE

When the head line is in its proper placement in rajas, you are safely moored in your objectivity. However, when your head line is pulled toward the heart, you can become emotionally vulnerable and reactive. You may speak without thinking and often say things you later regret. In this placement, your logic is superseded by your emotions when confronted or challenged. You must learn to remain calm and not overreact to people and situations.

PARTIAL DISPLACEMENT OF HEAD LINE INTO ZONE OF HEART LINE

During the period in your life when the head line deviates toward the heart line, you may be emotionally vulnerable and perhaps feel compelled to satisfy emotional desires, unmindful of their consequences. By making a conscious effort to think your way through your hurt feelings, you are able to place some distance between yourself and your emotions, thereby reestablishing your objectivity.

DISPLACED HEART LINE PULLED TOWARD HEAD LINE

When the heart line is in its proper placement in the realm of sattwa, there is a greater potential to express compassion and understanding. When the heart is pulled down into the rajasic area of the palm, feelings and emotions are cooled by the logic of the head; you become emotionally reserved and distant with a tendency to analyze everything. The heart should be allowed to express itself without rationalizing. Compassion and empathy need to be cultivated. Your mind will overrule your emotions to the degree that your heart line is displaced toward the head.

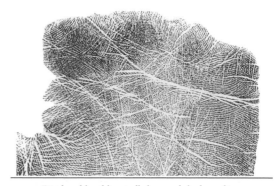

Displaced head line pulled toward the heart line.

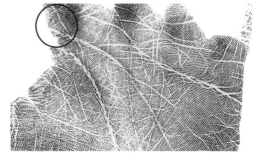

Partial displacement of head line into zone of the heart line.

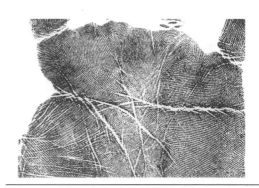

Displaced heart line pulled toward the head line.

Partial Displacement of Heart Line into Zone of Head Line

This formation is similar to complete displacement into the head-line zone, except that the duration is shorter. During the period in your life when the heart line dips toward the head line, your mind can be unnecessarily cautious, restricting the expression of your feelings. The duration of this temporary condition is indicated by the length of the displaced section of the heart line.

Branching and Connecting Heart and Head Lines

When the heart and head lines are joined together by branching lines, there is a short-circuiting of energies. This configuration indicates that your emotions and reason may interfere with each other's ability to function. Your reasoning is emotionally governed rather than objective, and the intuitive nature of your feelings can be restricted by overrationalizing. You may be unreceptive to good advice and out of touch with your intuitive capabilities. For restoring your peace of mind and ability to discern properly, relaxation techniques are helpful.

Branch of Heart Line Joining Head Line

A branch of the heart line going toward the head line indicates a short-circuiting of your intuition at the age indicated by the origin of the branch. You may feel compelled to make a dramatic move in your personal life regardless of the implications. For example, your feelings may be triggered such that you enter into an intense relationship with no awareness of the consequences; or you might try to reestablish contact with someone from the past who has proven to be incompatible. As this branch indi-

cates an overly impulsive nature, you should make a conscious effort to think through your decisions.

Partial displacement of the heart line into zone of the head line.

Branching and connecting heart and head lines.

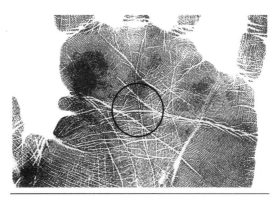

Branch of heart line joining the head line.

HEART LINE AND HEAD LINE PARTIALLY CONNECTED

This formation produces a short-circuit in faculties of reason and feeling, at times resulting in emotional reactions when objective reasoning is required. At other times, there may be a tendency to rationalize feelings, causing misunderstandings in relationships. You need to avoid extremist behavior and take care to channel your intensity properly.

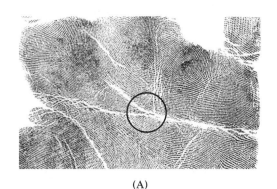

(A)

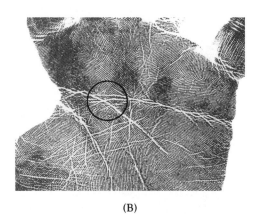

(B)

(A) Head line connecting with the heart line and (B) heart line connecting with the head line.

BLENDED HEART AND HEAD LINES

Sometimes we find a complete blend of the heart and head lines. This produces an intensity that results in an emotional and intellectual short circuit. You may have a tendency to be obstinate, forthright, and single-minded. However, positive lines and signs of the hand allow you to channel this intensity so that you can achieve success in whatever you endeavor. Without this support, you may be ruthless and insensitive to the needs of others. Regardless of the situation, your emotions are so entangled with your reason that your response is unpredictable. The result is an erratic, often blindly stubborn reaction, untempered by logic. When you try to have a rational discussion, you may become sidetracked by your feelings. And in situations that call for a sensitive, empathetic response, you may destroy the moment by making an inappropriate remark.

Maintaining a sense of inner peace can be challenging when the lines of heart and head are joined. In this case, you should work at developing positive lines and signs in the palm. By learning to avoid extremist behavior, you can

Blended heart and head lines.

develop a partnership between your reason and feelings to meet life's challenges.

Significance of Nature of Lines That Form the Quadrangle

The nature of the lines of heart and head—whether they are round or straight—determines how you use your reason and feelings.

CURVED HEART AND HEAD LINES FORMING QUADRANGLE

Rounded lines show a flexibility in attitude, as well as a give-and-take approach toward relationships. A round or curved line relates to infinity—a continuous recycling of energy—as opposed to a straight line, which implies rigidity and a resistance to being replenished. When the heart line curves, it is an indication that you want to incorporate love into your life. A curved head line shows that you are open to others' ideas and are compassionate to their trials. In contrast, a straight heart or head line is a sign of a more unbending and unforgiving nature.

Curved heart and head lines forming the quadrangle.

STRAIGHT AND PARALLEL HEART AND HEAD LINES

Straight lines are an indication of a tense, unyielding temperament. A curve in either the head or the heart line shows we have a release valve for the tension seen by the other straighter line in the quadrangle. We have a degree of receptivity in our character that can be appealed to. Straight parallel lines, however, indicate an extremely independent, unyielding, and defiant temperament, as the rigidity indicated by each line intensifies the inflexibility shown by the other. An intense nature may be detrimental to maintaining a long-term harmonious relationship. If you have this formation you need to make a conscious effort to understand your partner's feelings and needs and to make compromises where appropriate. In this way you can become more flexible.

Straight and parallel heart and head lines.

CURVED HEART LINE, STRAIGHT HEAD LINE

When you are in touch with your emotions, you experience an awareness of your feelings. The challenge, though, is when you try to express these feelings through words or deeds. A curved heart line signifies emotionally sound and sincere intentions. However, since your straight

Curved heart line with straight head line.

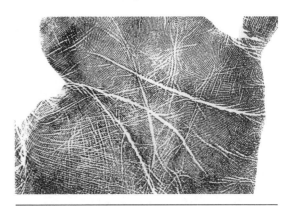

Straight heart line with curved head line.

head line indicates a straightforward and abrupt manner, your behavior may not represent your true feelings, and misunderstandings may occur. If you keep in mind that others can only respond to your intentions as they are revealed through your behavior, you can learn to modify your behavior to reflect your inner feelings.

STRAIGHT HEART LINE, CURVED HEAD LINE

A curved head line shows that, intellectually, you can be reasonable, understanding, and responsive in your dealings with others. However, a straight heart line suggests a narrow, unyielding range of feelings that may interfere with your ability to be flexible when issues touch you personally. In a relationship, you might be broad-minded and generous in neutral matters, but you become rigid, demanding, and self-centered when matters affect you personally. You should make an effort to be more loving so that your outward behavior has the support of emotional maturity.

WISDOM MARKINGS INSIDE QUADRANGLE

A wisdom marking, such as a cross, star, or square, appearing within the quadrangle is the stepping-stone to a higher level of awareness. Wisdom signs appear in this area as a result of

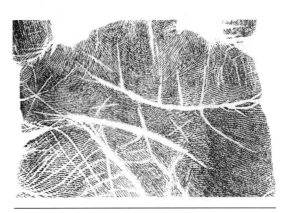

Wisdom markings inside the quadrangle.

the integration between your faculties of reason and feeling. They show that you are actively working toward reaching a greater level of understanding.

EMPTY QUADRANGLE

A quadrangle that has no lines or wisdom signs signifies that you are so preoccupied with everyday practical concerns that you may not realize your full spiritual potential. An absence of signs indicates that there is no dynamic interaction taking place between reason and emotion that can lead to a deeper understanding of life and

Empty quadrangle.

your place in the universe. You can learn to grow positive markings in the quadrangle if you make a conscious effort to learn about yourself. For example, instead of just asking "Am I good at my job?" you might also ask "How do I feel about my job?" and "Does it contribute to my self worth?" "Does it serve others?" You could set aside a time each day for self-reflection—meditating, writing in a journal, or whatever puts you in touch with your inner being.

Too Many Lines Inside Quadrangle

Too many criss-crossing lines within the quadrangle reflect confusion. You tend to create unnecessary complications for yourself by doubting

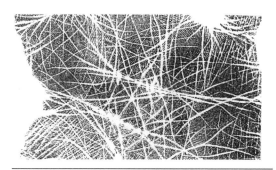

Too many lines inside the quadrangle.

both what you think and what you feel. Thus you may find yourself attracting untimely conflicts. Your energies may become dispersed or exhausted through not being focused. Definite efforts must be made to overcome uncertainty and indecision.

SIGNIFICANCE OF ORIGIN, TERMINATION, AND FORMATION OF HEART LINE

The placement of the heart line origin provides information about what motivates your desire for a loving relationship—your inner emotional nature. The point of termination shows the outward manifestation of that inner template—the extent to which your reaction to life's experiences modifies it positively or negatively. The formation of the heart line in between these poles indicates the process whereby you learn to express your potential for loving.

Heart Line Origins

Upward Origin

The ideal heart line originates with an upward curve. An upward direction indicates that your heart is open. Feelings of optimism, trust, and confidence are incorporated in matters of love.

Downward Origin

When the heart line turns down toward the head line, your heart is ruled by a cautionary, questioning, doubting nature. By making a conscious

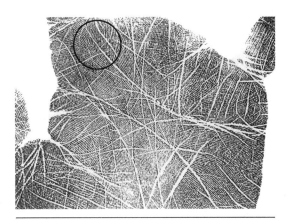

Heart line upward.

Forked heart line.

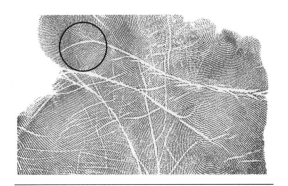

Heart line downward.

THREE-PRONGED FORK ORIGIN

A three-pronged heart-line origin indicates you can be known for your loving, compassionate disposition with tremendous spiritual insight used for the welfare of humanity. Especially when all three branches are of equal length, this origin denotes talent, success, and possibly even fame.

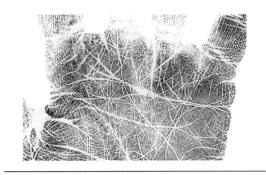

Three-pronged heart line.

effort to reach out to others, you can learn to become more open and spontaneous.

FORKED ORIGIN

A heart line originating with a fork shows intensity in the feeling and expression of love and suggests an inclination to be soft and sensitive in matters of the heart. It shows that you are sincere and trustworthy with a willingness to give and a desire to share in relationships. However, your extremely idealistic nature makes you prone to disappointment when your expectations are not met, and your intentions may often be misinterpreted by your partner.

SINGLE LINE ORIGIN

A heart line originating with a single line, rather than a fork or branches, signifies a need to learn to express your feelings, especially those relating to love. You need to cultivate a spirit of sharing more fully.

Single line origin.

Conclusion

The ideal heart line originates on the mount of Jupiter, crosses the mounts of Saturn and Sun, and ends on the mount of Mercury. It is important, therefore, for you to understand what each of these mounts reveals about your nature, particularly with respect to the origin, formation, and termination of the heart line.

SIGNIFICANCE OF HEART LINE ORIGINATING ON JUPITER

The Jupiter mount represents the ego—how we see ourselves and our unique purpose in the world. It reflects the strength of the intellect and its ability to be focused in our chosen direction. It is the mount of ambition. When Jupiter energy is operating well in our lives, we see our unique gifts working within a larger whole. However, with a negatively developed Jupiter mount there is a danger of becoming so preoccupied with success, recognition, status, competition, and influence over others—in other words with defining who we are by what we do—that we feel isolated from others and our own loving nature. A positive Jupiter influence shows that while we see ourselves as having a special role to fulfill, we don't lose sight of the fact that as human beings we are all interconnected. Our satisfaction comes not from being applauded by others, but from the joy of being of service to them. Jupiter then becomes the mount of generosity.

Ideally, the heart line turning upward on Jupiter reflects an ease of expression in contrast to the constricted feeling indicated by the heart line turning down toward the head line. The upward-turning heart line reflects someone who gives spontaneously without any conditions, while the person with a downward-turning heart line is subject to too much thinking.

The origin of the heart line on Jupiter shows a generous, expansive, jovial nature. Because you are able to express the love you feel in your heart completely, you feel contented, self-contained, and free. You are able to love without making demands and without conditions.

The golden rule advises us to love our neighbors as ourselves; in other words, we are not separate from each other. Perfect love consists of giving without looking for recompense and accepting others without judgment. The heart line originating on Jupiter indicates a capacity for pure love. While you love others without making demands, the very fact that you see others' shortcomings, albeit compassionately, can make you difficult to live with. Others may feel you are demanding positive changes—which, by example, you are, although not as a precondition to love. Ironically, this profound capacity to love may lead to misunderstandings as others may feel inadequate by comparison, or suspicious of your motivation.

Jupiter Origins

In order to examine all the possible origins on the mount of Jupiter, it is helpful to horizontally divide the mount into three worlds—sattwa, rajas, and tamas, and then to vertically divide it into the "world within" and the "world without," sometimes called the inner and outer worlds.

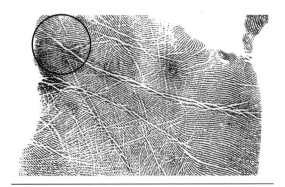

Sattwic world within.

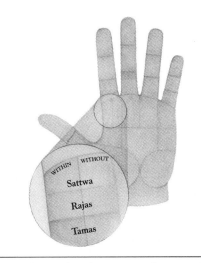

Key to locating heart line origins on the mount of Jupiter.

Heart Line Originating on Sattwic World of Jupiter

SATTWIC WORLD WITHIN

The heart line originating deep within the sattwic world of Jupiter reflects a commitment to loving others without reservation. It connects the two worlds of Jupiter—inner and outer. Unconditional love is not simply an idealized concept but is practiced in everyday living. Traveling across the entire length of the Jupiter mount, this heart line reflects a profound dedication to love unconditionally. With this for-mation, you tend to attract individuals with shorter heart lines who may test your resolve to love without reservation, but who are, nonetheless, receptive to developing an authentic relationship.

SATTWIC WORLD WITHOUT

This origin speaks of the same high standard of love expectations as above, except that your firm dedication to loving may not be as completely rooted as in the previous case. There is an intense desire to find a compatible partner. Although you realize that you should not be too demanding, you may, in actual fact, be overly sensitive in your expectations of your partner,

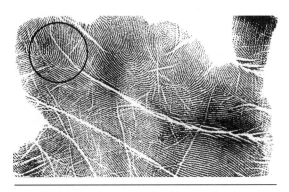

Sattwic world without.

becoming somewhat aloof when faced with human imperfections.

Heart Line Originating on Rajasic World of Jupiter

The heart line originating on the rajasic world denotes all the same Jupiterian qualities as the origin from the sattwic world. The differences between an inner world and outer world origin are also the same. You are sincere, affectionate, loving, faithful, amiable, and very enthusiastic and idealistic in matters of love. Although you

try to overlook the faults of your beloved, you may find this hard to do as you demand perfection and like to place your partner "on a pedestal." You can be forgiving in matters of love but do not easily forget. The heart line on the rajasic world, however, denotes a greater emphasis on social interaction. You are not as concerned with intellectual preoccupations, nor as open to hurt when your intentions are misunderstood.

You want your mate to be well-respected in society, independent, and mutually committed to a strong, positive cause. However, there is a tendency to see no reason to share your energy and waste your time unless there is a common goal or purpose to be achieved. You must be careful not to let jealousy, anger, envy, or frustration arise when your partner's behavior is not completely synchronized with your own.

FORK ON SATTWIC WORLD OF JUPITER

This shows intensity in the feeling and expression of love. It denotes that you are trustworthy and sincere. You have extremely idealistic expectations that are difficult or impossible to meet. However, you have such an intense longing to

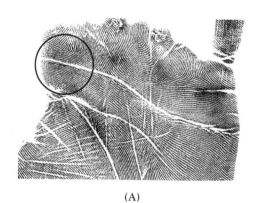

(A)

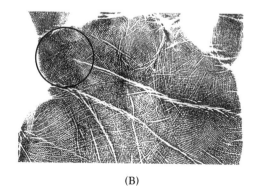

(B)

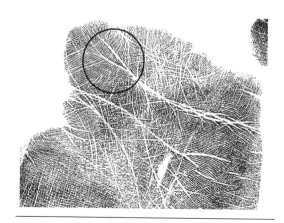

(A) Rajasic world within. (B) Rajasic world without.

Fork on the sattwic world of Jupiter.

form a life-long bond that you may overlook your partner's failings and hence be prone to disappointment when he or she falls short of your expectations.

FORK ON RAJASIC WORLD OF JUPITER

You are easily drawn to magnetic, beautiful, or handsome partners whom you tend to idealize. You can, however, make the mistake of falling in love with someone with whom you have little in common. You are peace-loving and gentle. Often able to sublimate the sensual side of love, you may be drawn to the contemplative life.

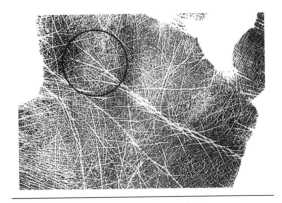

Fork on the rajasic world of Jupiter.

THREE-PRONGED FORK ON SATTWIC AND RAJASIC WORLDS OF JUPITER

Three branches of equal length denote a very successful individual. There is a possibility of international name and fame—if a good Sun line is also present. It can also denote excellence in art, science, medicine, philosophy, or religion. Very talented, compassionate people often have this form of line. Samudrik Shastra texts state that this form of heart line is found in the hands of saints and enlightened yogis with tremendous spiritual insight.

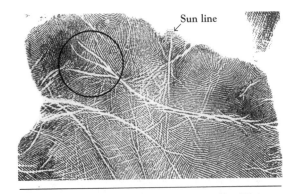

Three-pronged fork on sattwic and rajasic worlds of Jupiter.

Heart Line Originating on Tamasic World of Jupiter

A heart line originating on the tamasic world of Jupiter shows that you have idealistic expectations in matters of love and sex; however, the straight heart line suggests that you can go to extremes in love. You may be irrational, possessive, and jealous. Although you seek perfection in your mate, you may not be willing to make the

Heart line originating on the tamasic world of Jupiter.

necessary sacrifices to attract your ideal partner. When your expectations are not fulfilled, you may feel nervous, intense, and frustrated. This heart line origin does not point to harmonious love relations. However, other positive lines and signs in the hand may help to moderate the extremist tendencies suggested by this origin.

Significance of Heart Line Originating on Mount of Mars Negative

This is the mount related to primitive instincts for survival, one of which is the fight-or-flight instinct. We have, however, the ability to choose whether to be governed by our reflexes or exercise control over our behavior. The Mars mount reveals the degree to which our nervous systems are able to handle negative stimuli. We may decide that we should be reasonable and not respond negatively to what is going on around us. However, we may not have a strong enough nervous system to support this positive intention.

In the early formative years human reasoning isn't yet developed. Children are at the mercy of their emotions. They haven't yet learned to objectify things. When a parent is too tired to play, a child can feel hurt and angry. She doesn't understand that her parent's mood isn't directed at her personally, but is the consequence of perhaps having had a bad day at work. The mount of Mars negative reflects accumulated emotion for things we experienced but could not explain. We can, however, learn to process our experiences with empathy, forgiveness, and understanding. Mars then relates to the degree to which we temper our instinctual impulses toward anger, frustration, anguish, revenge, and sarcasm.

HEART LINE ORIGINATING ON MARS NEGATIVE

The heart line originating on Mars negative indicates a tendency to be cautious and defensive. Because you are unable to trust your own goodness, you cannot believe that anyone is as selfless and loving as they appear to be. A Mars heart-line origin suggests that in order to protect yourself from being surprised and hurt by the failings of others, you constantly scrutinize their behavior. This caution leads to a lack of spontaneity, which makes it difficult to enter into an open, loving relationship.

Unfortunately, a negative dynamic can be set up whereby you can become so fearful of being hurt and unloved that you don't recognize true affection when it is offered. Your partner becomes hurt by your pessimism and suspicion and may turn away from you. The very thing that you fear becomes a reality.

Despite your suspicious nature, you have high expectations of others. Whenever your partner fails to live up to these expectations you feel anger, resentment, and jealousy. You construct an intellectual pattern of analysis and evaluation, leaving no room simply to feel love for your partner.

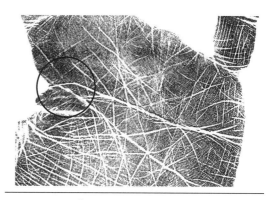

Heart line originating on Mars negative.

It is difficult to break this pattern of fearful-ness and mistrust. The fact is, however, that no one is perfect and hurt is an inevitable part of human relationships. We have no control over how others behave, but we can make choices about our own behavior. Once you stop being critical, demanding, and suspicious, you become more relaxing to be with; consequently, you create opportunities for love to enter your life.

The deeper the origin of the heart line on Mars negative (i.e. the tamasic world), the more indication there is that you may respond physically to your disappointments. Mere criticism or vocal expression of your feelings of resentment isn't enough; you may resort to physical violence.

In short, a heart line originating on the sat-twic world of Mars negative reflects a predisposition to thinking negatively. If it begins in the rajasic world, you will express your frustrations verbally through scolding, criticism, and sarcasm; if it begins in the tamasic world, you may respond physically.

HEART LINE REACHING JUPITER BUT TURNING DOWN TOWARD HEAD LINE AND MARS NEGATIVE

Since your heart line draws on the energy of two mounts—Jupiter and Mars negative—you display some of the characteristics of both. You are cheerful, loving, sincere, and sensitive, as the path across Jupiter suggests. However, you also have a tendency to store up negative emotion, which is sometimes expressed at inappropriate times—a trait associated with Mars negative. Although naturally idealistic, you may have a tendency to judge others critically, which can result in eventual disharmony in your relationships with others. You have a strong desire to love unconditionally, but cautious tendencies

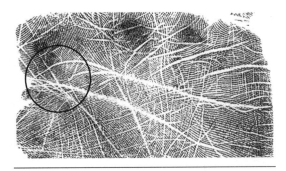

Heart line reaching Jupiter but turning down toward the head line and Mars negative.

may make you fearful and untrusting. You may attract a potentially ideal mate; however, your constant criticism may either drive the person away or cause him or her to fulfill your worst fears. If you can learn to be brave enough to trust more you may encourage your partner to be more loving.

Significance of Heart Line Originating on Mount of Saturn

Saturn relates to our philosophical nature. Its influence in our lives brings caution, responsibility, discipline, and seriousness. Saturn represents a quiet, deeply analytical nature that leads to a profound understanding of life.

The heart line originating on the mount of Jupiter needs the support of Saturn. The wisdom and discipline reflected in Saturn enhance the love and compassion of Jupiter. A Saturn origin shows that while the wheels of evolution are in motion, it is difficult for you to feel spontaneous and giving since you lack the influence of Jupiter's unconditional love. You are self-absorbed. Perhaps you are wrestling with the implications of a profound life experience; possibly you are engaged in unraveling the mysteries of life. At any rate, your personal needs come first, before you are willing to engage in any relationship that necessitates a generous, selfless, surrendering nature.

You may, therefore, appear cold at times. Your disapproval may prompt others to keep their distance—and so a negative pattern of aloofness and reserve could be perpetuated.

The closer the heart line is to Jupiter, the more sensitive you are to the people and the environment around you. The closer the heart line is to Saturn, the more constrained your emotions are as you take on some of the reserve and caution of this distant planet.

SINGLE LINE ORIGINATING AT CONJUNCTION OF SATTWIC WORLD OF JUPITER AND SATURN

A commonly found heart line origin is between the mounts of Jupiter and Saturn. With this origin you are faced with an emotional dilemma in that you are on the threshold of change. Although you are used to behaving in a reserved and cautious manner, you feel the need to be more spontaneous.

A single line originating at the conjunction of Jupiter and Saturn denotes the coolness of Saturn and the idealism of Jupiter. You do not demand such a high degree of perfection in your mate as does someone who has a true Jupiter origin. Neither do you demonstrate your feelings in public. Although reserved, you have strong and deep feelings. You believe strongly in reason and faithfulness. When placed in a situation of responsibility, you do your best to perform your duty faithfully and sincerely.

In many cases a branch extends from this formation to the center of the Jupiter mount. This indicates a release from the overcautious and matter-of-fact nature of Saturn, moving toward the more expansive expression of Jupiter. If a long line of union is also present, a desire to open up and share your feelings with another is indicated.

FORKED HEART LINE: ONE BRANCH TO CENTER OF JUPITER, ONE BRANCH TO SATTWIC WORLD OF CONJUNCTION OF JUPITER AND SATURN

This heart-line formation is considered to be one of the most positive. It shows a blend of idealism with reason. Guided by a strong sense of

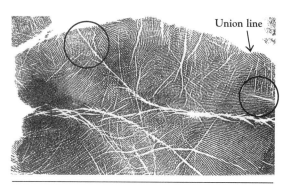

Single line originating at the conjunction of the sattwic world of Jupiter and Saturn.

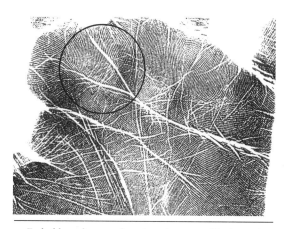

Forked heart line: one branch to the center of Jupiter and one branch to the sattwic world of the conjunction of Jupiter and Saturn.

spiritual conviction, you are equally aware of your material duties. This formation denotes a potentially successful love life. You are expressive, demonstrative, sincere, and faithful. You enjoy a calm and quiet home life.

Heart Line Originating on Sattwic World of Saturn

A heart line originating on the sattwic world of Saturn represents a deliberate, restrained, aloof nature. The "world within" of Saturn suggests that you are more realistic in your relationships than the "world without," which suggests a lack of seriousness and sincerity. However, the latter heart line is very rarely seen.

The heart line originating on the sattwic plane of the world within shows a quiet, analytical nature. You tend to view life in subjective terms, often lacking the capacity to put yourself in someone else's shoes. In order to have successful relationships, you should endeavor to be less inward-turning, and to express appreciation and affection for others spontaneously and with enthusiasm.

Heart Line Originating on Rajasic World of Saturn

A heart line originating on the rajasic world of Saturn shows that you have an independent nature that leaves little or no room for acceptance of another person's priorities. You tend to react according to whatever suits you, when ideally your expression of love should reflect compassionate, thoughtful, genuine concern. Until you develop these qualities, your emotions will feel suffocated.

The shorter heart line originating on the world without on the mount of Saturn is rarely seen. In such a case, the ability to express love is limited by priorities of a material nature. You long for financial security in your partnership, and seek out relationships that will increase your material comfort.

Heart Line Originating on Tamasic World of Saturn

A heart line originating on the tamasic world of Saturn denotes attachment to the physical

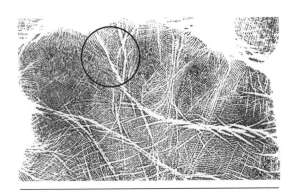

Heart line originating on the sattwic world of Saturn.

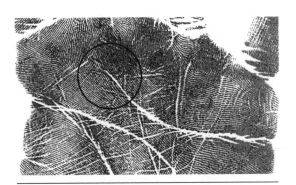

Heart line originating on the rajasic world of Saturn.

world, and hence reveals an egocentric need for comfort and pleasure. Since the heart line is the gauge that reflects emotional interaction, this formation indicates your inability to develop a profound loving relationship due to your insistence on personal pleasure. You tend to prefer sexual satisfaction to romantic involvement in relationships.

Since this heart-line formation is close to the head line, you are very determined in love, but for selfish reasons. You are demanding and like to be flattered. If your emotions are aroused and you believe you are in love, you will do almost anything to possess the object of your desires. However, you tend to lose interest once you have obtained what you want. With this heart line there is a definite need to learn to be more compassionate.

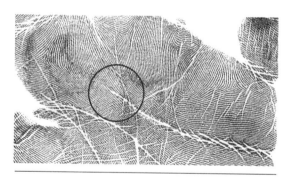

Heart line originating on the tamasic world of Saturn.

Unusual Combinations

Heart Line Originating on Tamasic World of Sun

This heart line configuration is not commonly found. The heart line originating on the mount of Sun indicates an impulsive nature. You tend to lack emotional depth and therefore your relations are instinct-bound. You are physically and sexually very alive and put a high priority on pleasure, passion, and fun. You are given to sudden outbursts of emotion—both high and low. To counteract this tendency you should seek the company of an exemplary companion or associate.

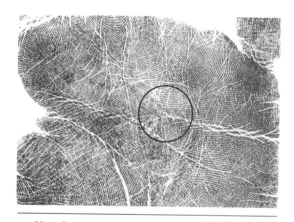

Heart line originating on the tamasic world of the Sun.

Complete or Near Absence of Heart Line

Although extremely rare, the absence of a heart line can be an indication of any of the following: a) utter intensity of intellect has taken over your sentiments to the point of total ruthlessness, blind stubbornness, and irrationality; b) you are governed by negative emotions (as in the case of the blended heart and head lines); c) the organic health of your heart is at risk as a result of uncontrolled negative emotions.

Occasionally, a person without a heart line may have a girdle of Venus. This minor line suggests that the mind is creating a channel through which inherent sensitivity can become manifest.

Although you may have tremendous difficulty in expressing love for others, you are able to respond to idealized representations of love and may perhaps be an inspiration to others.

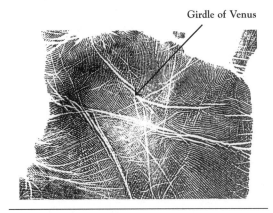

Blended heart and head lines with the presence of a girdle of Venus.

DOUBLE HEART LINE

The double heart line shows an excessive need for emotional interaction. This constant bombardment of your emotions creates confusion, which makes it difficult for the mind to exert the appropriate balance. You find it difficult to

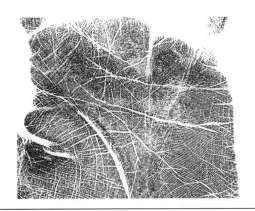

Double heart line.

develop lifelong bonds with your partner or associates, and tend to have difficulty maintaining your commitment to causes in which you truly believe. You need to cultivate devotion as an antidote to allowing your emotions to rule you.

Heart Line Terminations

SIGNIFICANCE OF HEART-LINE TERMINATION

Although palmistry is not intended to be a compilation of predictions about the events of a person's life, we all experience two inevitabilities: birth and death. The soul enters the physical realm at birth with a set of character traits and tendencies. As we grow through childhood, adolescence, and adulthood, we develop relationships and pursue a career and lifelong goals that reflect our particular nature. Hopefully, we learn and grow from our experiences so that when we die we are wiser and more evolved.

The heart line, being sattwic in nature, relates to how completely we are attuned to our soul throughout life. The origin of the heart line shows the inherent attitudes that underlie our potential for expressing love. The termination of the line relates to the point at which the soul leaves the body in death. Ideally, we strive to become loving, compassionate, and accepting in our relationships with others. If we succeed, then at the end of life, we are calm, open, and serene as our soul leaves the body.

Our progress is reflected by the features of the heart line as it passes across each of the mounts. The five digits of the hand are divided into the inner and outer worlds: the thumb

(Venus) and Jupiter finger make up the inner; the Sun and Mercury fingers make up the outer; the Saturn finger (like the quadrangle between the heart and head lines) forms a neutral zone between the two worlds. The ego, part of the inner world indicated by Jupiter, is ruled by the mind. Our attitude toward sharing, part of the outer world indicated by Sun, is ruled by the heart. Enlightenment, part of the outer world indicated by Mercury, occurs when we transcend body, mind, and emotions. This happens at death; however, if we can learn to see ourselves and all other living things as part of a whole—that is, as pure spirit—we are able to transcend without actually leaving our physical bodies.

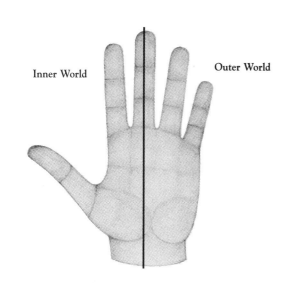

The five digits of the hand are divided into the inner and outer worlds.

The natural tendency of your ego is to make you believe that you are an isolated entity. The ideal heart line, crossing the palm from origin to termination, parallels the process by which the conscious mind becomes aware of the spirit. This awareness brings the realization that you are whole. You no longer feel the need to search outside yourself for completeness because you are already complete. Until you become fully conscious of your self, you cannot understand that you do not exist as a separate self.

While there are many origins for the heart line, reflecting the manifold varieties of human nature, the termination of the heart line, which always occurs at the outside edge of the hand, reflects the universality of death. Although the heart line's termination occurs in the area of the palm that designates age sixty-three and on, it signifies the quality of your nature as you approach death at whatever age it occurs. We often think of old age as the time of wisdom; however, a child with a terminal illness may exhibit acceptance, serenity, and compassion beyond his or her years.

The heart line, as with all lines of the hand, performs a dual role: sequential as well as simultaneous. It provides a map of the events of life in chronological order, as well as an indication of lifelong attributes and tendencies. The heart line's termination is an indicator of how close to the ideal of love we are actually expressing throughout life, as well as during the time indicated by the termination. The Vedic texts teach that, in death, our consciousness exits the physical body. However, we can be aware of transcending the physical not only at death but throughout our lives. The degree to which we recognize ourselves as more than finite beings determines the quality of our expression of love. For example, you may have a partner who has been unfaithful. You show unconditional love when you are willing either to let your loved one go or welcome your partner back without recrimination because you desire that he or she find happiness.

Location of Heart-Line Termination

The ideal heart line, originating on the inner world of Jupiter, crosses the mounts of Saturn and Sun to terminate on the outer world of Mercury. The features of the heart line show the evolution of our feelings, from personal to transpersonal and from egocentric to universal, as we move through the four time zones from childhood to old age. Each of the mounts traversed by the line corresponds to one of the four elements—water (Jupiter), fire (Saturn), air (Sun), and ether (Mercury). These elements are equally important, but move from the physically contained to a state of freedom.

From the amniotic waters of birth we grow—testing our strengths and weaknesses as we move through childhood and on to adolescence. Matured in the fires of Saturn, we leave behind our childish ways as we structure our lives to survive in the adult world. In middle age, having established our place in the world, we begin to sense through the element of air a freedom of expression that transcends the confines of structured patterns of thinking and feeling. In old age the element of ether heralds the potential for liberation as our consciousness anticipates detaching from the world to reconnect with the pure love of spirit.

IDEAL HEART-LINE TERMINATION: ON BORDER OF MOUNTS OF MERCURY AND MARS POSITIVE

This termination reflects a balanced disposition in matters of love and affection, feelings and emotions. In India, the Mercury mount is referred to as Buddha, signifying enlightenment. Mars positive is known as the warrior mount, signifying courage, persistence, and supportiveness. A heart line terminating at the conjunction of these two mounts reflects the ability to use the energy of Mars positive to bring the enlightenment of Mercury into relationships. It shows that you are sensitive to the needs of your loved ones and have the stamina to fulfill those needs.

In addition to the wisdom associated with enlightenment are the qualities of wit, spontaneity, humor, light-heartedness, and articulateness. That is why so many of our spiritual leaders, such as the Dalai Lama and Mother Teresa, have combined intense dedication to serving humanity with childlike delight in simple things, which is the mark of being able to love unconditionally.

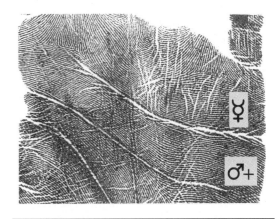

Ideal heart line termination on the border of the mounts of Mercury and Mars positive.

Variations in Termination

HEART LINE PULLED UP ON MERCURY

The heart-line termination curving upward into Mercury shows that you lack the commitment represented by Mars positive. You become flighty. Wit, spontaneity, and freedom, usually positive qualities, provide an escape from dealing with the responsibilities of day-to-day living. In your relationships you may be unable to hear the layers of feelings behind your partner's words. Your relationships, therefore, are likely to be somewhat shallow. By insisting on maintaining your freedom, you may actually create tension for yourself. You need to recognize that loving requires energy and that you need to surrender some of your Mercurial freedom if you want to build a long-lasting, committed, and mutually attuned relationship.

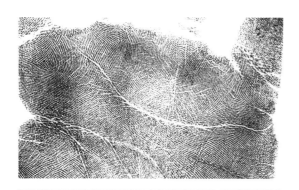

Heart line pulled up on Mercury.

HEART LINE PULLED DOWN ON MARS POSITIVE

The heart-line termination curving downward into Mars positive shows a tendency to be self-oriented.

The energy of Mars the warrior, whose concern is the well-being and protection of others, needs the balance of the outward- and upward-looking Mercury to keep from becoming overly demanding, possessive, and controlling. Since unconditional love requires the greatest degree of commitment and self-sacrifice, we need the energy of Mars positive to support us in our commitment to the ideal. Without the vision of a profound, loving relationship, that energy can be misdirected: it can be turned inward to become self-serving. For example, a father who wants the very best for his child may hold her hand when she crosses the street to protect her from danger. However, when he insists on choosing her friends and career, justifying his behavior as "wanting only the best for her," he may be acting from self-interest. You need to guard against imposing your own personal agenda, and learn to listen to the needs and desires of your loved ones.

Heart line pulled down on Mars positive.

EQUAL BRANCHES UPWARD AND DOWNWARD ON MOUNTS OF MERCURY AND MARS POSITIVE

Branches equally formed above and below the heart line on Mercury and Mars positive reflect a karmic connection between you and your family. You have a profound desire to care for your children and are capable of expressing your love and affection for them. Your children may cause you pain and worry; however this is all part of the dynamic of a healthy, interactive human relationship. Your children are likely to care for you in turn with the same warmth and affection. Feathered branches show the capacity to expand your consciousness to view humanity as one large family that you can love with generosity and open-heartedness. Since these branches occur at the termination of the heart line, signifying age sixty-three and on, they reflect the capacity to form open, caring, nonjudgmental relationships with those who touch your heart— particularly children and younger people—in the latter part of life.

Ideally, there should be two or three branches above and below the heart line. More than this number is an indication that your emotional energy is being dissipated.

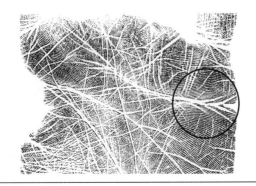

Equal branches upward and downward on the mounts of Mercury and Mars positive.

BRANCHES UPWARD ON MERCURY

Branches on the upper side of the heart line on the Mercury mount, or branches that are more developed on the upper side than those on the lower, indicate that you are conscious of your desire to love your children and to give them whatever you can. You may, however, be oblivious to the concerns associated with an interactive relationship, as you are too self-contained. You may be happy in your love for your family but, because you are not fully aware of your responsibility to be attuned to their needs, the relationship is not a fully developed one. For example, a father may work overtime to provide for the physical needs of his family and be quite happy and content to do so, but he may overlook the fact that his wife is depressed and his children would like him to spend more time with them. If you have this characteristic, you should make a conscious effort to be more aware of the expressed or implied needs of your loved ones.

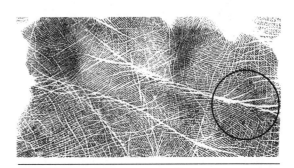

Branches upward on Mercury.

BRANCHES DOWNWARD ON MARS POSITIVE

Better-developed branches on the lower side of the heart line as compared to the upper side suggest that you are overly preoccupied with the lives of your family members, particularly your children. Your energy is constantly depleted by anxiety and sadness, especially when your advice is disregarded and your help is either taken for granted or not reciprocated. You can improve your emotional health if you learn to give what you can, meet your filial responsibilities, then let go, relax, and enjoy life.

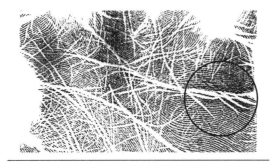

Branches downward on Mars positive.

Significance of Heart-Line Formation

LONG HEART LINE

A long heart line shows an ability to be deeply committed to all relationships. The heart line that crosses the palm indicates that you are in tune with your feelings; you are confident, demonstrative, spontaneous, and self-reliant. Although capable of forming loving relationships, you are not emotionally dependent on others for your

happiness. The longer the heart line, the greater the desire to seek lasting love.

Although generally a positive formation, a long heart line must be seen in the context of its overall formation. For example, a long, straight heart line indicates a tense, possessive, unyielding nature; a long, curved heart line, however, signifies a more open, sincere, and emotionally sound temperament.

Long and imbalanced heart-line formation.

SHORT HEART LINE

A short heart line indicates that the fulfillment of your practical needs and desires takes priority over emotional depth in your relationships. You have a preference for physical passion, comfort, and sensual pleasures. With less endurance for

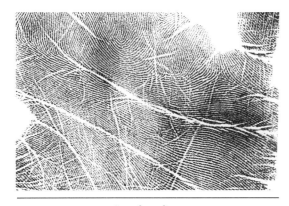

Long heart line.

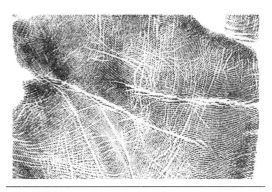

Short heart line.

giving, affairs of the heart—relationships, love-making, and so on—tend to be short-lived. By understanding that pleasures are temporary while the state of joy is lasting, you can learn to choose emotional fulfillment over physical gratification.

CURVED HEART LINE

A curved heart line reflects a joyful, idealistic disposition with a desire for harmony. Your heart is governed by a spirit of sharing, giving, and loving. You reconcile problems or misunderstandings peacefully with a calm, empathetic attitude. You have the ability to accommodate the needs of others with tolerance and endurance.

Curved heart line.

OVERLY ROUND HEART LINE

An overly round heart line shows a tendency to be too sentimental. In matters of the heart, you are ruled by your emotions, which can be extreme. Your ability to make clear decisions may be compromised and judgments may be colored by emotional rather than rational preference. You should guard against hasty, emotionally biased impressions; impulsive behavior may reinforce emotional vulnerability. You need to balance your enthusiasm for love with com-

mon sense in order to build and maintain long-lasting relationships.

Overly round heart line.

STRAIGHT HEART LINE

A straight heart line denotes a direct, forthright approach to love. You have rigid expectations of others and become impatient with any behavior that fails to meet your immediate demands. You may be prone to emotions such as jealousy, envy, or possessiveness. By developing awareness of the circumstances and limitations of others, and by accommodating their preferences, you can learn to develop more compassion and empathy.

Straight heart line.

WAVY HEART LINE

A wavy heart line is indicative of unpredictable, unsteady emotions, so that at times your reason prevails and at others your emotions overwhelm you. These fluctuating emotions present difficulties in maintaining healthy, long-lasting relationships. By making a conscious effort to temper your emotions with reason, you can become more constant in matters of the heart.

Wavy heart line.

NARROW HEART LINE

The width of the heart line suggests the degree of refinement in your emotional nature. The ideal heart line—neither too wide nor too narrow—maintains a balance between awareness and

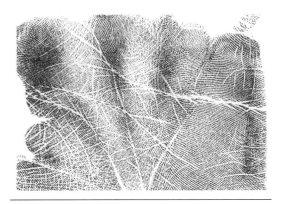

Narrow heart line.

action. This heart line shows that you are sensitive and responsive to the needs and desires of others.

An overly narrow heart line shows a tendency to be too inward. For example, although you may be extremely sensitive to everything around you, you become overwhelmed and lack the stamina to deal appropriately with your feelings. You may seek refuge in the realm of aesthetics as an alternative to participating in the real world of interpersonal relationships.

WIDE HEART LINE

A wide heart line indicates an extroverted nature hampered by a lack of sensitivity. You have the energy to show outward affection for your loved ones yet you often act inappropriately because you may not be in tune with the needs of your partner. You can refine your relationships and your heart line by becoming more aware of your partner's needs.

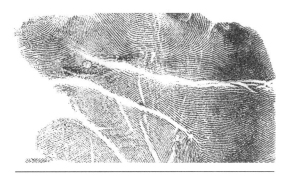

Wide heart line.

DEEP HEART LINE

The depth of the heart line shows the degree of conviction in matters of love.

A deep heart line reveals an ability to enter into a profound, long-lasting, harmonious, mutually satisfying relationship.

Deep heart line.

SHALLOW HEART LINE

The shallower the line, the less interest you have in a deeply committed relationship. Your tendency is to continue a relationship only as long as you are deriving physical and emotional pleasure and benefit from your partner. In order for you to deepen your relationship, you must be more deeply concerned with your partner's needs.

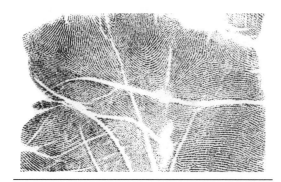

Shallow heart line.

EVEN HEART LINE

An even heart line shows consistency of formation. It reflects a self-disciplined, self-controlled, and self-confident nature in matters of love. You are receptive to the needs of others and have the ability to maintain long-lasting relationships with steadiness of heart.

Even heart line.

MIXED HEART LINE

A mixed heart line may be wide at one part, narrow at another, or generally level with the occasional "pothole." It reflects that you are not enjoying a fully contented emotional life, and that consistency in emotions needs to be cultivated.

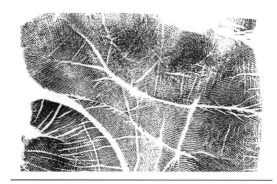

Mixed heart line.

FREE-FLOWING HEART LINE

A heart line without any interruptions denotes a free flow of energy that enables you to negotiate affairs of the heart with ease and joy. The emotional strength suggested by a free-flowing heart line also promotes physical health, vitality, and optimism.

Free-flowing heart line.

DOT ON HEART LINE

A dot on the heart line depicts stress on the heart caused by conscious or unconscious temporary worries. You may be identifying with hurt feelings from unreciprocated affection in a past relationship. In order to restore health, you need to make an effort to not dwell on past disappointments.

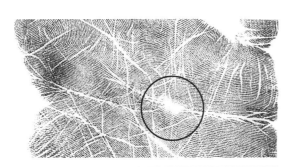

Dot on heart line.

ISLANDS ON HEART LINE

Islands on the heart line are an indication of short- or long-term conflicts, stress, or discomfort. They may point to an organic health condition that can adversely affect your emotional health and vitality. A precise understanding of the effect depends on the location, size, and number of islands found on the heart line, as determined by the following examples.

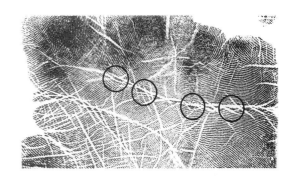

Islands on the heart line.

SINGLE ISLAND ON JUPITER

An island on the heart line on the mount of Jupiter suggests a conflict caused by family surroundings in early childhood that continues to affect your emotional well-being. If both hands are affected, the memory may persist throughout

Single island on Jupiter.

the course of your life. However, if the heart line continues smoothly after the island, you have the potential to overcome this difficulty. You should make a conscious effort to put the events of the past in the proper perspective with all their karmic implications in order to move forward unencumbered.

SINGLE ISLAND ON SATURN

An island on the heart line on the mount of Saturn indicates sadness. You have a tendency toward being reclusive, and you may feel withdrawn as far as your emotions are concerned. You need to learn how to express rather than repress your emotions.

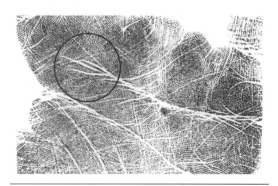

Single island on Saturn.

SINGLE ISLAND ON SUN

An island on the heart line on the mount of Sun reveals a blockage. Some form of hurt or disappointment is causing you to lack spontaneity in expressing your emotions. When others fail to meet your expectations you should not allow yourself to be hurt by this, but instead try to develop a more forgiving nature. You should guard against compensating for your disappointment. If you observe your lifestyle, you may dis-

cover poor eating, sleeping, and sexual habits that are interrupting the smooth flow of energy.

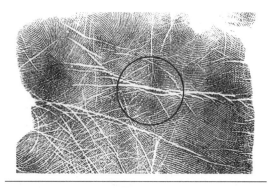

Single island on Sun.

SINGLE ISLAND ON MERCURY

An island on the heart line on the mount of Mercury reveals an emotional blockage caused by an inability to communicate in love and relationships. You need to make a conscious effort to be more open; otherwise the pressure of not being able to express your feelings may adversely affect your health.

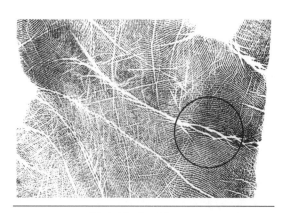

Single island on Mercury.

SEVERAL LARGE ISLANDS ON SUN AND MERCURY

Several large islands on the Sun and Mercury mounts show a tendency to nurse hurt, anger, or violent emotions. If not corrected, this may eventually lead to erratic, destructive behavior. An attitude of tolerance toward others and acceptance of your own inadequacies will help rebuild your emotional balance. The tendency to harbor negative emotions may also result in a careless attitude toward diet and exercise that, in turn, could cause circulation problems, blood toxicity, or high blood pressure. Proper diet and exercise will help rebuild your stamina.

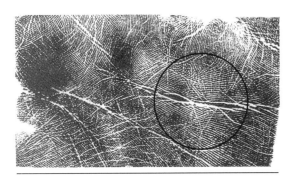

Several large islands on Sun and Mercury.

CLUSTER OF SMALL ISLANDS ON SUN AND MERCURY

A cluster of small islands on Sun and Mercury denotes a tendency toward oversensitivity and sadness. Emotional stress and failure in relationships may cause depression, leading to indifference to proper eating habits that, in turn, can result in malnutrition. If care is not taken, this neglect may lead to low blood pressure. Periodic medical checkups are advised. You should make a conscious effort to overcome sadness, anxiety, and brooding over past mistakes. Freeing your-

self of negative patterns gives you more energy to express love.

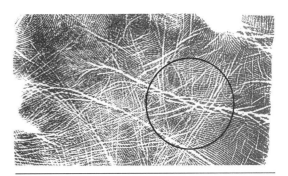

Cluster of small islands on Sun and Mercury.

CONTINUOUSLY CHAINED HEART LINE

A continuously chained heart line denotes that you are ruled by anxiety, uncertainty, and fear of commitment, which manifest in unsteady behavior. You may be prone to attracting problematic relationships. Before entering any new relationship, you should strive to create a calm, reflective environment in which self-inquiry can take place. Once you have a clear understanding of why you attract certain relationships, you can make better-informed choices. You will become more confident in your associations with others, more trusting, and more capable of commitment.

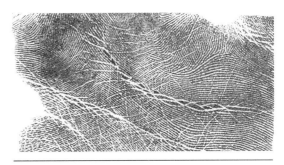

Continuously chained heart line.

BROKEN HEART LINE

A broken heart line generally relates to disappointments in love. A broken line indicates a particular event or radical change in attitude, which can cause an emotional change at the age where the break occurs. It is possible to heal a broken heart line. If the break indicates an earlier trauma in love, you can transform the effects of the disappointment; if the break points to a future circumstance, you can modify your attitudes in preparation.

In some cases, the break may be related to a physiological heart condition. Periodic medical checkups are advised to rule out this possibility.

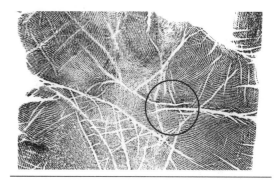

Overlapping heart line.

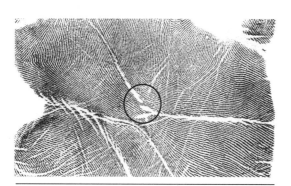

Broken heart line.

CONTINUOUSLY FRAGMENTED HEART LINE

A continuously fragmented heart line indicates difficulty in making decisions related to affection and love. Your emotions tend to fluctuate as fear, confusion, and insecurity continuously overwhelm more positive feelings. You find it hard to trust others as a result of having absorbed many shocks and experienced failure in intense relationships. You may be conscious of the need for a change in attitude, yet find it hard to discipline your emotions. You need to form associations with inspiring, uplifting, and

OVERLAPPED HEART LINE

Overlapping lines on the heart line are similar to breaks, although the effects are experienced less intensely. Overlapping indicates a gradual change occurring during the time of your life indicated by the overlap. You have the potential to overcome failures or disappointments in love, and are supported in your struggle to change your attitude toward love. You may enter this transitional period feeling despondent; however, you become increasingly optimistic as you prepare to begin something new.

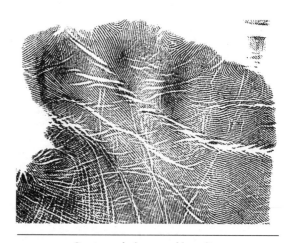

Continuously fragmented heart line.

encouraging individuals who can strengthen your resolve to change.

INTERFERENCE LINES CROSSING HEART LINE

Interference lines indicate conflict that may impede the smooth flow of your emotional life, or suggest a challenge that needs to be overcome. At the particular age indicated by the interference crossing the heart line, you may experience serious difficulties in your relationships. A heart line that becomes stronger after the interference line shows that you have learned from the experience and have matured as a result. A broken heart line, or one that appears fainter after the interference, shows difficulty in accepting the shock, failure, or rejection. If you can embrace the idea that experiences come in life not to destroy you but to make you a deeper, more empathetic, forgiving, and understanding individual, you can come to see interference lines as blessings in disguise. By becoming broad-minded and letting go of negative attachments, you free yourself to move forward.

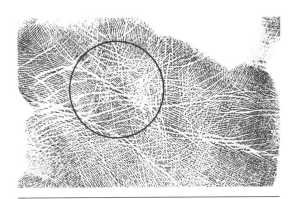

Interference lines crossing the heart line.

ASCENDING MINOR BRANCHES OF HEART LINE

A minor branch ascending from the heart line shows that you want to open your heart and extend yourself to others. The positive, sattwic attitude reflected by the ascending line shows that you can attract members of the opposite sex who are helpful and inspiring.

Ascending minor branches of the heart line.

DESCENDING MINOR BRANCHES OF HEART LINE

A minor branch descending from the heart line shows that you have a tendency to be emotionally vulnerable. You succumb to infatuation in your search for someone to satisfy your emotional, sentimental, and sexual needs. The

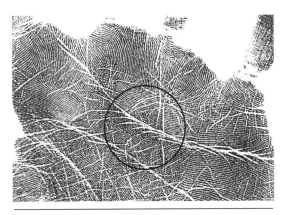

Descending minor branches of the heart line.

descending branch implies a subjective, tamasic inclination toward emotionally charged unions that may ultimately result in your feeling dependent, out of control, and empty.

Many branches—whether ascending, descending, or both—indicate an extremely emotional nature. You may be gullible, unstable, unpredictable, and overly sentimental.

Conclusion

Once you are able to decipher the code embedded in your heart line, you will learn much about your capacity for loving. By growing and refining this line, you can alter your personal magnetism and, consequently, improve the interpersonal relationships in your life.

3
Finding Love in the Hand

Although the heart line is the primary indicator of your loving disposition, other features in the hand reveal your receptivity toward cultivating a meaningful relationship. This chapter looks at several key factors that speak of your sensitivity, and your degree of emotional attunement to the needs of your partner, friends, and associates.

Before we consider the specific features that relate to loving relationships, we need to explore the underlying concept of magnetism and its inherent duality.

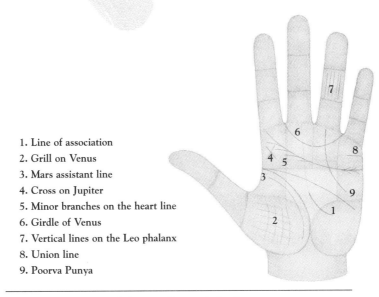

1. Line of association
2. Grill on Venus
3. Mars assistant line
4. Cross on Jupiter
5. Minor branches on the heart line
6. Girdle of Venus
7. Vertical lines on the Leo phalanx
8. Union line
9. Poorva Punya

Indicators of love in the hand.

THE NATURE OF MAGNETISM

Within each of us is a dance of opposites—more or less harmonious—of equal and complementary yet opposing forces. We all have both masculine and feminine aspects, reason and emotion, soul and mind. To develop and maintain a successful relationship, we have to resolve our own dualities by recognizing seeming opposites as aspects of a greater unity. We can then embrace another and enter into the bond of partnership, which is greater than the sum of its parts.

At some distant time and place the universe began. The most widely accepted theory proposed by many scientists is the big bang. According to the big bang theory the universe originated billions of years ago in an explosion from a single point of nearly infinite energy density, sometimes known as the cosmic egg. The metaphysical counterpart to this scientific theory is that, in the beginning, before any physical manifestation, there was

The opposite forces of attraction and repulsion, positive and negative, masculine and feminine are represented here in the yin–yang symbol.

an unmanifested yet omniscient creative intelligence whose "thought" gave birth to the physical three-dimensional reality of our universe. This creative energy—variously called the prime mover, the universal intelligence, the creator, or God—became manifest in the physical universe as two opposite forces: attraction and repulsion, positive and negative, masculine and feminine.

THE CENTER OF THE UNIVERSE

In Hinduism, the center of this physical universe is a neutral place referred to as Vishnunabhi. It is through this point that the original unmanifested creative energy is manifested in physical form, known as the dual forces of Shiva and Shakti.

Hindu metaphysics views the entire universe as one gigantic magnet held together by the two oppositing forces of Sun and Moon, or Shiva and Shakti. From the macro universe, through the solar system, to each of us as individuals, right down to the very smallest subatomic particle, all things have the positive and negative energies of a magnet. And, like any magnet, our universe—and everything within it—has a central neutral zone that is neither positive nor negative, but rather, like the original "source point" or center, is nonmagnetic. No matter how many times a magnet is split in half, it retains its opposite poles, and its neutral center. Thus, at the heart of everything lies this neutral zone, called Vishnunabhi.

This dimensionless point plays a key role in evolution as the source through which the universe was created. If we see the purpose of life as the quest to free ourselves from duality and become one with the source of creation, then it would seem logical to reverse the process. The closer we come to accessing this central point by merging the two poles of Shiva and Shakti (a reverse big bang), the closer we come to regaining our spiritual heritage.

THE PENDULUM THEORY

The formations of the mounts indicate the progress of our spiritual evolution. Each mount represents a particular portfolio. An overdeveloped mount may indicate too forceful a nature: you are too Shiva in your expression. You need to become more Shakti to find balance. An underdeveloped, or Shakti, mount may indicate too passive a nature: you need to be more Shiva to regain your equilibrium. In either instance, you are subject to the laws of duality; you have lost your balance and have temporarily lost your objectivity, a trait associated with your spirit, or soul. Humans can spend lifetimes alternating between these two extremes. The pendulum theory in palmistry suggests that an abuse or overuse of the energy of a mount (overdeveloped) results in the lack of the same energy (underdeveloped) in a subsequent incarnation. Our goal is to reach the still center point where Shiva and Shakti become one, and consequently, where our nature is in harmony with the divine.

SUN AND MOON: THE COSMIC DANCE

The Sun lies at the center of the solar system and, through its magnetic force, maintains all the planets in their orbits. The Moon receives and reflects the light of the Sun. In Hindu astrology, the Sun is known as the "king," and the Moon as the "queen." Each plays a fundamental role in matters of love. In palmistry, the hand is seen as a microcosm of the solar system, containing all the planetary bodies represented by the mounts. Similar to the planetary bodies in astrology, the mounts of Sun and Moon in the hand provide us with significant information about our ability to give and receive love.

The Hindu concept of Shiva and Shakti embodies the divine union of opposites. The god Shiva is lord of reason; the goddess Shakti embodies emotion. In the study of palmistry, the Sun and Luna are the representations of the archetypes Shiva (creator) and Shakti (receiver). The Sun represents Shiva, or the father, and Luna represents Shakti, the mother. One aspect of the Sun is the soul or atma; another is the active discriminating energy of reason or wisdom. One aspect of the Moon (Luna) is the mind, or *manas*, that interprets the physical world through the senses; another is feelings or emotion.

Through the limitations of the five senses, the mind—represented by Luna—receives limited information about the physical universe. Beyond the limitations of our senses lies the Sun, or soul, which is, by virtue of its transcendence over the senses, limitless. A calm, balanced mount of Luna indicates that you have achieved an objective state of mind. You create within yourself a peaceful environment that enables you to recognize your true nature, which is soul. When you become still, free from conflict, you can begin to receive the light of the Sun.

The peace you begin to experience, having learned to control the senses, is necessary if you are to intuit and merge with the qualities of the Sun. The more neutral or impersonal you are, the easier this task becomes. This does not mean that you lack concern or care. On the contrary, through the absence of the emotional complications associated with a personalized and subjective Luna, you become free to experience pure unconditional love for others.

A balanced Luna shows that you can allow yourself to be guided by the Sun, or soul, within. If you free yourself from identification with your personal impressions, fears, and biases, what remains is a secure self-knowledge and empathy toward the needs of others.

Any imbalance in the mount of Luna reflects an inability to remain consistently calm and objective. This can result in a lifetime preoccupied with reacting emotionally to the changing events in your life. We often hear it said that the only certainty in life is change. But although you may see yourself as having little or no control over the changing events of your life, you can control your perception of these events, and hence your reaction to change. Rather than seeing change in a linear fashion, from positive to negative or the reverse, you can choose to perceive life as cyclical—moving from birth, growth, maturity, and death to rebirth. You may develop to the point of no longer identifying your experiences as good or bad, as successes or failures. If you view each "negative" experience as an opportunity for growth and understanding, and each "positive" event as an invitation to exercise discrimination and responsibility, you will eventually reach the point where you no longer think in terms of whether something affects you positively or negatively. You can simply learn to be. Once you refuse to be at the mercy of your sensory impressions and your emotional responses to them, you can attract and maintain a happy, healthy, and long-term relationship.

Luna, Goddess of Creativity

Luna signifies our desires, emotions, and sense impressions. Ideally, it should be approximately two-thirds the size of the neighboring mount of Venus, thus indicating steadiness, depth of character, and an ability to make a commitment.

Luna, the Moon goddess, signifies our desires, emotions, and sense impressions.

IMBALANCED LUNA

An underdeveloped or overdeveloped Luna indicates that your view of reality is skewed. An underdeveloped Luna shows that you are

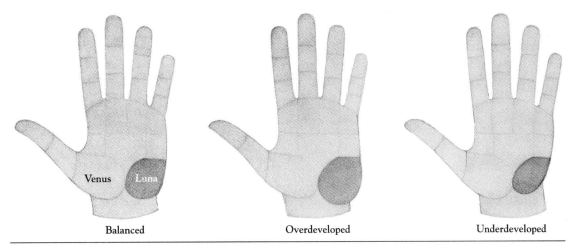

| Balanced | Overdeveloped | Underdeveloped |

Luna: the three levels of development. Ideally, the mount of Luna is two-thirds the size of Venus.

anxious, apprehensive, and insecure. An over-developed Luna indicates a tendency to be excitable and overstimulated, and consequently impulsive and subjective in interpreting events.

OVERDEVELOPED LUNA

An overdeveloped Luna indicates that you are being flooded with sensory stimulation. Because you crave excitement, you may have difficulty coping with day-to-day reality, often escaping into a fantasy world. You may be self-absorbed and, therefore, unable to perceive the needs of your partner.

Carol: Imaginary Lover

Carol, a woman in her early twenties, dreamed of having a relationship. As she had an overde-veloped Luna, however, it was easier for her to simply create an imaginary lover. Every evening at the supper table she would describe to her family romantic encounters that she was having with a mysterious new boyfriend. As the weeks passed her older sister grew suspicious, wondering why Carol hadn't as yet introduced him to the

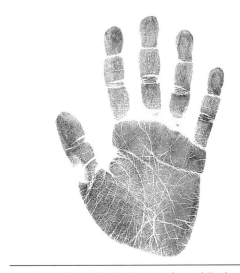

Carol's overdeveloped Luna indicates difficulty coping with day-to-day reality.

family. To satisfy her curiosity, she followed her sister to college. Again at suppertime, Carol recounted stories of her lover. This time, her sis-ter confronted her and said, "But you were alone all day." Carol finally admitted that there wasn't anyone, and that the relationship was com-pletely imagined.

With such a strong head line and well-developed Luna, Carol was encouraged to channel her creativity into writing. The focus and concentration required to do so anchored her in reality and helped her to differentiate between fact and fantasy. She went on to graduate, and eventually introduced a real boyfriend to her family.

UNDERDEVELOPED LUNA

In contrast, an underdeveloped Luna (less than two-thirds the size of Venus) suggests a person whose senses are frozen. With this formation you avoid excitement and seek security in familiar routine. Your response to life lacks enthusiasm and joy. By making a conscious effort to value the beauty of life moment by moment, you can learn to defrost the senses; you can begin to enjoy a life where "the glass is half full, not half empty."

Nelly and Ambrose: A Honeymoon Story

Nelly has an underdeveloped Luna. Her husband, Ambrose, has a balanced one. Ambrose discovered his wife's apprehensive nature on their honeymoon when he thought it would be romantic to drive to a secluded mountain lodge, well known in the area as a honeymoon retreat. Nelly was terrified. She was preoccupied with the possibility of accidents, attacks by wild animals, and so on. Although both experienced the same environment, Ambrose, a balanced Luna, saw the isolated spot as romantic if spiced with a hint of danger. Nelly, an underdeveloped Luna, perceived the retreat as a disaster in the making. For Ambrose the glass was half full, but for Nelly, half empty.

Nelly

Ambrose

Although Nelly and Ambrose experienced the same environment, for Ambrose, the balanced Luna, the glass was half full, but for Nelly, an underdeveloped Luna, it was half empty.

WHIRLPOOL ON MOUNT OF LUNA

A whirlpool found on Luna is an indication of subjectivity. In personal relationships, you tend to interpret events solely from your own emotional perspective. You may imagine hurts and insults and become inappropriately sad and withdrawn. Similarly, your perception of events may trigger defense mechanisms that lead to

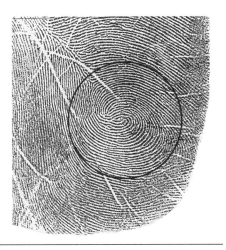

A whirlpool on Luna is an indication of subjectivity.

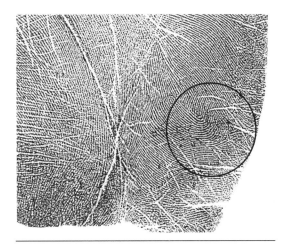

Maureen's whirlpool on Luna indicates over-dramatization.

arguments and resentment instead of a willingness to resolve misunderstanding. By learning to discriminate between what has actually happened and what your imagination has added, you can become more objective, thus minimizing stress in your relationships.

Maureen: A Taste for Drama

As a child and as a young adult, Maureen was chronically moody. She blamed her condition on the fact that her brother, who had been diagnosed as manic depressive, had babysat her for many years. The whirlpool on her Luna indicates that her overly dramatic response to the effect of his condition upon her was causing her depressed state. She, not her brother, was responsible for her moodiness. Once she realized that she was using her brother's situation as an excuse for her own moods, Maureen, over time, learned to rechannel her innate creativity into writing screenplays.

Destiny Line

The destiny line shows the ability to channel emotional energy into some purposeful or creative activity. A positive destiny line shows that you have the determination and enthusiasm to pursue a lifelong purpose. Having a goal frees you to incorporate a loving relationship into your life, rather than searching for someone to fill the empty space produced by your own lack of direction. It is important to maintain a good destiny line through constant focus, vigilance, and dedication.

Mary: Lost Destiny

Mary was a successful and glamorous television executive. David was attracted to her exuberant and dynamic style. She was self-confident and enjoyed her work in the media immensely. When David entered her life, however, she found herself paying more attention to him than to her work. Soon she became demanding and

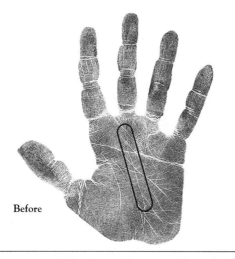
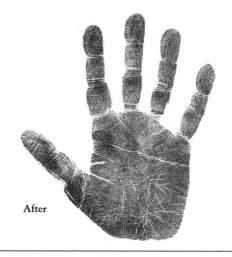

Before   **After**

Mary's prints show a strong destiny line before she met David and no destiny line afterward.

dependent. Her work, which previously had given her personal satisfaction, began to suffer. David, who was originally attracted to her dynamism, felt repelled by her all-consuming need for his entire attention.

Notice the strong destiny line in the "before" print, and its absence in the "after" print. Mary lost her job. David broke up the relationship, and Mary became so despondent that she even contemplated suicide. It was recommended that she rekindle her sense of purpose in life in order to reestablish her destiny line. Mary almost lost everything—including her life—before she realized that she could sustain a profound, loving relationship without abandoning her own focus.

LINE OF ASSOCIATION JOINING THE DESTINY LINE

A line of association joining the destiny line indicates that you have a vocation and are receptive to someone entering your life who can participate with you in accomplishing a mutual goal.

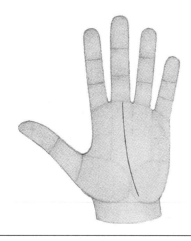

A destiny line from Luna.

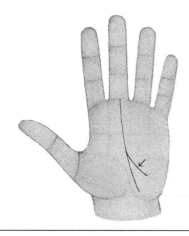

Line of association.

Gina: A Working Relationship

Gina, an ambitious sales representative, loved her job. She fell in love with her company's advertising director and they began living together. The love they shared provided stability, incentive, and mutual support. They found great pleasure in planning and executing new advertising strategies for their company.

The line of association shows a receptivity to having a relationship—one that through friendship instills a sense of help, support, and inspiration. This supportive line indicates your receptivity to a partner with whom you can have a shared understanding of life.

ing someone into your life who may interfere with your ambitions. You may be deflected from your intended goals through subterfuge, scandal, or some other form of conflict.

A destiny line that becomes stronger after a break or interference caused by a line of association indicates that, through mutual understanding and acceptance, you can overcome the difficulties encountered at the beginning of your relationship. It may also indicate a difficult relationship that challenges you to take command of your destiny. As a result, your life's direction becomes more focused.

Gina's line of association.

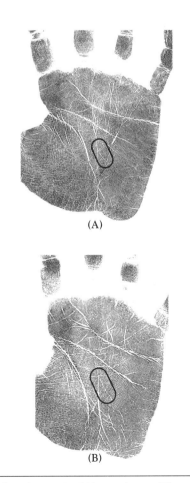

(A)

(B)

The line of association (A) strengthens or (B) weakens the destiny line.

LINE OF ASSOCIATION STRENGTHENING OR WEAKENING DESTINY LINE

The line of association should merge with the line of destiny. It should not break, cross over, or obstruct it in any way. Ideally, the destiny line is strengthened by this line.

A line of association that breaks or weakens the destiny line at the point where they meet shows that you may leave yourself open to allow-

Meg: Adversity Strengthens

Drawn together by a mutual interest in philosophy, music, and literature, Meg and Charles seemed to have a happy marriage. A child was born and Meg took a leave of absence from her teaching job. Repeated infidelity on Charles's part at this time caused the relationship to end. Charles was unwilling to pay alimony and insisted that Meg return to work full-time. Although devastated by the divorce, Meg threw herself wholeheartedly into her teaching, deriving immense satisfaction from her students. Before long, she was recognized as a leader in her field.

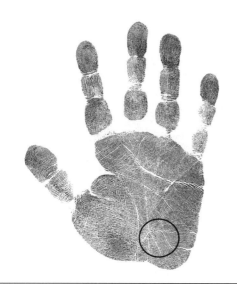

In Meg's case, her destiny line grows stronger even though it meets with an interference line at the point where the line of association joins it.

Sun, God of Light

BALANCED SUN

The Sun, as a reflection of our soul, indicates that the impossible can happen. The characteristics manifested by the Sun defy logic.

Explorers, inventors, and saints—all those who have done what was said to be impossible—have positive Sun energy indications in their hands.

Norma: A Psychic Healer on the Battlefield

Norma, a gifted psychic, served as a medic during the Second World War. On the battlefield she used her intuitive "X-ray vision" to accurately assess the injuries of the wounded. Norma's highly developed Sun mount with a star, combined with her straight Sun finger, indicates her dedication and compassion for helping and serving others. It also shows her exceptional concentration and focus, which helped her to establish a link with her intuitive, extrasensory ability.

IMBALANCED SUN

The development of the Sun indicates the degree to which you are in touch with your spiritual nature. Ideally, a balanced Sun finger reaches the middle of the sattwic phalanx of the

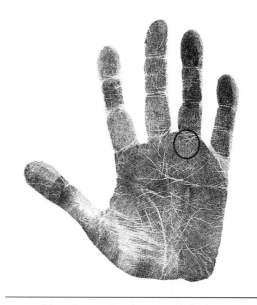

Norma's strong Sun finger, mount, and star.

Saturn finger. An underdeveloped Sun shows that you lack self-reliance and can, at times, feel incompetent. An underdeveloped Sun also indicates that you lack awareness of your spirituality. You must learn to trust the soul energy within; that is what gives you the competence to reach your goals.

An overdeveloped Sun indicates a charismatic, powerful nature; however, it may also point to a need to guard against egocentricity. You may be tempted to believe that power emanates from within you instead of understanding that you are simply a channel for spiritual energy. If the finger is straight (not twisted) and lines and signs of wisdom are present on the mount, the long Sun finger indicates a growing attunement with your spiritual self. You show that you are becoming a vehicle through which your thoughts and actions can be guided by the perceptive intuition of your soul.

By recognizing that you are the trustee of spiritual energy, and not the source, you can experience a childlike joy, knowing that it comes from a higher power within.

OVERDEVELOPED SUN

An overdeveloped Sun indicates that you are intelligent, charming, and dynamic. You may have forgotten, however, that your unique and powerful way of expressing yourself is meant to be used for the good of humanity and not for self-aggrandizement. In its extreme, an overdeveloped Sun shows that you must guard against conceit, arrogance, and manipulation of others for your own ends. You should make an effort to leave space for others to enter your heart.

UNDERDEVELOPED SUN

An underdeveloped Sun, in contrast to a balanced one, shows that you can make simple tasks impossibilities. You may feel suffocated in your isolation and feel overwhelmingly incompetent. A lack of enthusiasm and poor self-image are the result of feeling disconnected from

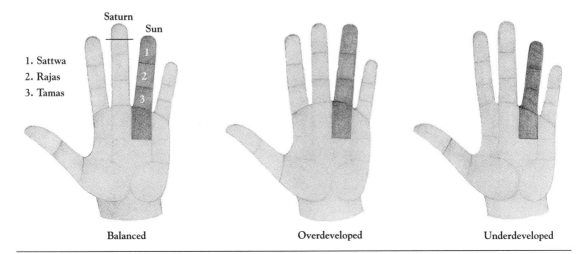

Balanced   Overdeveloped   Underdeveloped

The development of the Sun mount and finger shows to what degree you are aware of your spirit.

your spirit. You need to develop self-reliance, and trust that the intuition of your inner guidance (soul) will not fail you.

Jenny and Barbara: Student and Mentor

Great friends and coworkers for the past ten years, Jenny and Barbara complement each other's natures. Jenny, the youngest of a large family, left home when she was quite young and moved to France to find work in the film industry. In her first job interview, despite her lack of previous training or film experience, she convinced her prospective boss that he wouldn't be able to do without her. After one week, she was hired. Note the strong development of Jenny's Sun mount and finger.

Barbara grew up in a more protected and conservative environment. Her nature is more introspective and reserved than Jenny's, as shown in part by her smaller Sun finger. Together, Barbara and Jenny enhance each other's potential.

Although extroverted, Jenny needed direction and reassurance to help focus and channel her exuberant, dynamic energy. Barbara, already accomplished in her line of work, was able to help her friend and, in the process, find an outlet for her own creative expression—by helping to inspire Jenny to be proficient in the same field.

Lines and Signs on Mount of Sun

Lines and signs on the Sun mount indicate the degree of your conscious attunement to spiritual energy. They indicate whether you are prone to attract positive or negative circumstances, people, and events into your life. Positive lines and signs are usually found on a more balanced mount, which shows that you have already established an understanding of the nature of your inner spirit. The positive lines simply indi-

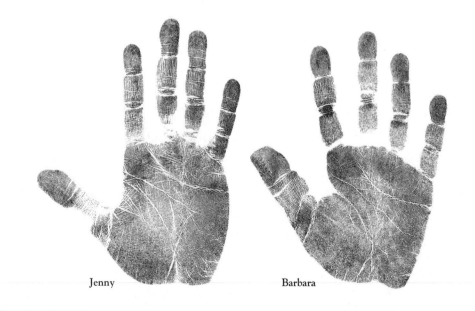

Jenny   Barbara

Jenny's Sun mount and finger indicate her expressive and outgoing nature. Barbara, in comparison, is more introspective and reserved, as shown in part by her smaller Sun finger.

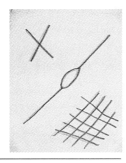

(Left) Positive lines and signs on Sun show that you have established an understanding of the nature of your inner spirit. (Right) Negative lines and signs on Sun suggest a degree of spiritual misalignment.

A single line of Sun shows that you can attract prosperity.

cate that you are now consciously and actively engaged in directing this energy for a specific purpose. You become committed to achieving goals that reflect the sharing, supportive, and humanitarian nature that this mount represents.

Negative lines and signs found on an imbalanced Sun mount suggest an inability to channel the Sun energy positively. These negative lines and signs suggest a degree of spiritual misalignment. Limited by the dictates of your ego or mind, you sometimes use your spiritual energy inappropriately, to your detriment.

SINGLE SUN LINE

A single line of Sun is a sign of magnetism, conscientiousness, and focus, showing that you are in contact with your heart, or atma. This line is also an indicator of your public persona. It shows that you are confident and decisive; you know what you want. Depending on your definition of success—whether it be happiness, money, or the realization of a lifelong dream—the Sun line shows that you can attract prosperity. In the magnetism created by your intensity of purpose, you draw into your life others who have similar goals. Although not an actual line of partner-

ship, the Sun line increases your potential to attract positive relationships into your life.

MULTIPLE SUN LINES

In contrast to a single line, too many Sun lines indicate a diffusion of energy. You have too many goals. This can result in your feeling scattered and unfocused. Multiple Sun lines indicate enthusiasm. However, you may be uncertain as to your long-term focus in life. As a result, you may attract someone into your life who may also be unclear about his or her goals. Conversely, you may attract a partner with a single Sun line who may draw you into his or her life because you lack priorities of your own.

Eddy and Louise: An Enterprising Relationship

Eddy had always known what he wanted: to establish a family-run empire in the clothing industry. It took him fifteen years to make his dream a reality. Steadily, from waiting tables to selling shoes, to opening a factory and selling his own line of sportswear, he became a millionaire. Eddy's single, strong Sun line shows that he is

Multiple Sun lines indicate a diffusion of energy.

as reflected by the presence of a Sun line, her indecision is also seen by the fact that she has too many Sun lines. While he waited tables, her husband was happy to put her through college, after which she found a job as a travel agent. As her husband's dream became a reality, she accepted a position as the company's full-time manager. Perhaps on account of Eddy's intensity and focus, Louise was drawn into his dream, and together they created a multimillion dollar enterprise.

STAR ON MOUNT OF SUN

A star on the Sun mount indicates a passionate, charismatic nature, one that is in tune with your inner being. The star draws upon the energy of the spirit to attract positive relationships, the realization of dreams—anything your heart desires. When you "wish upon a star," all things are possible.

in touch with his heart. He has no hesitation or doubt. He has faith and confidence and loves everything he does. This enthusiasm is reflected even in his company logo printed on the labels of each garment—a soaring eagle. In everything he did, Eddy believed himself successful. He never resented others' prosperity or thought of himself as poor. Instead, he saw others' success as an inspiration. If they could achieve their goals, then so could he.

Louise was a little more unsure of what it was she wanted out of life. Although fortunate,

The star on the Sun mount indicates that you are able to tune in to the universal unconscious. You recognize the underlying themes and issues that bind us all together in our humanity and our spirituality. The intuitive un-

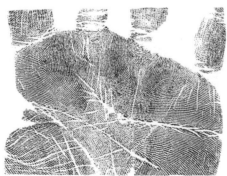

| Eddy | Louise |

Eddy's single, strong Sun line shows that he is in touch with his heart. Louise's indecision is seen by the fact that she has too many Sun lines.

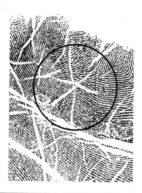

A star on the Sun mount shows that you can touch the hearts of others.

The star on Martin's Sun mount reflects his ability to tap into the hearts of thousands through his music.

derstanding indicated by the star manifests diversely in religious, political, and artistic individuals who, through their unique modes of expression, touch the hearts of all those with whom they come in contact.

Martin: A Star Is Born

Martin, a famous musician, recounted one of his first experiences playing before a large audience. On a warm summer evening he was scheduled to give an outdoor concert. As he walked toward the stage with his guitar in hand, he could hear his name being chanted by thousands of loyal fans who had turned out to hear him play. The star on his Sun mount indicates that he is able to tap into the hearts of thousands through his music.

CROSS ON MOUNT OF SUN

A cross on the Sun mount is a sign of indecision and doubt. Through your hesitancy, you may lose opportunities that could have resulted in bringing you success and contentment. This inability to make a commitment often causes you to make negative comparisons between yourself and others. The two lines that make up

the cross reflect an obstruction to the flow of spiritual energy. The cross shows mistrust in your intuition, and that is ultimately self-defeating. Since intuition is a manifestation of spirit, you must learn to trust that aspect of yourself that has greater comprehension than your mind does.

Robert: A Missed Opportunity

Robert, a young graduate student, was dating Vicky, a security guard. To him, she was the woman of his dreams. Both had the same wish

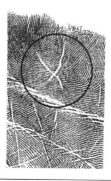

A cross on the Sun mount is a sign of indecision and doubt.

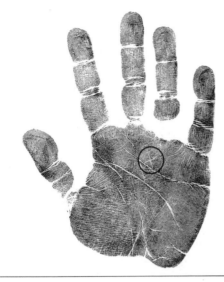

The cross on Robert's Sun mount reflects his inability
to make a decision.

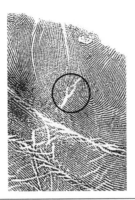

An island on the Sun mount shows a blockage
in magnetism.

to retire early and sail around the world; however, they realized this could only happen if one of them won the lottery. Despite their precarious financial situation, Vicky pressed Robert to marry her. Robert was reluctant to make a commitment and kept putting her off. Frustrated by his indecision, Vicky ended the relationship, much to his sadness. She later married her supervisor. A year later, Robert saw on television that Vicky had won the Irish sweepstakes and was sailing around the world with her new husband.

Robert's cross on his Sun mount reflects his inability to make a decision. He lost both the woman he loved and, ironically, the realization of his lifelong dream.

ISLAND ON MOUNT OF SUN

An island on the Sun mount indicates blockages in magnetism. You may feel isolated from others. This often results in a poor self-image and a belief that no one can really love you for who you are.

You may become overly defensive in your insecurity and repel the very people you are trying to attract. And so, by default, those you do attract are likely to be negative influences in your life. You tend to act inappropriately, provoking the criticism of others, which makes you even more defensive—and the cycle continues. In its extreme, this could even lead to your involvement in a public scandal.

By recognizing the cause of your difficulties through objective self-analysis, you can "erase" the island.

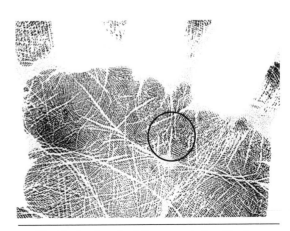

The island on Jonathan's Sun mount isolates him from
his own loving nature.

Jonathan: The Lonely Millionaire

Jonathan, a multimillionaire, did not believe his wife could really love him for himself. His lack of trust in his own appeal prevented genuine communication between him and his wife. The island on Jonathan's Sun mount reflects a blockage that isolates him from his own loving nature.

Lines on Leo Phalanx

Similar to the division of the hand into sattwa, rajas, and tamas regions, each finger, consisting of three phalanxes, is also divided into sattwa, rajas, and tamas. Straight, deep, vertical lines on the middle phalanx of the Sun finger—sometimes referred to as the Leo phalanx—indicate

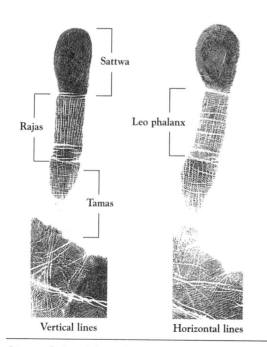

Vertical lines   **Horizontal lines**

Lines on the Leo phalanx indicate the nature of your relationships with your associates.

the nature of your relationships with your associates. They show that you have affection for those you work with, are inspired by them, and are committed to realizing common creative goals. Vertical lines on the Leo phalanx represent innocent and childlike qualities of the soul: you have fun working on projects with others. These lines indicate a degree of personal magnetism and attunement to the world around you.

Horizontal lines crossing the Leo phalanx show that you may be unable to express your feelings for others as much as you would like.

Laurette and Lionel: Two Big Suns

Laurette and Lionel were happily married for fifty years. Both came from large families: she had thirteen brothers and sisters and he had eight. Losing his father at an early age forced Lionel to leave school and earn money for the family. As the eldest son, it was his responsibility to look after his younger brothers and sisters. After having met at a funeral of a mutual friend, Laurette and Lionel fell in love, were married, and went on to have a large family themselves.

Later, Lionel was diagnosed with terminal cancer. As he lost weight, Laurette would take in his pants at night so when he put them on in the morning he would not realize the weight loss. When he weighed himself, she would slip her foot onto the scale so that he would not be alarmed by how much he had lost. Although he felt deeply for Laurette, Lionel was never able to express his affection for her verbally. Instead, he would leave small love letters for her—in the fridge, in her cupboard, everywhere—to surprise her. Throughout the year following his death, Laurette kept finding little notes of affection and inspiration from him.

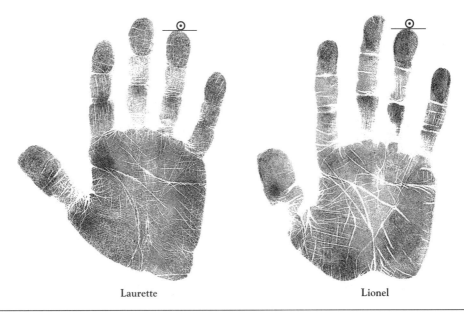

Laurette   **Lionel**

Laurette and Lionel's Sun fingers reflected their commitment to the same ideal of serving, sharing, and simply loving each other and their large family.

Their long Sun fingers reflected their commitment to the same ideal of serving, sharing, and simply loving each other and their large family. After Lionel's death, Laurette found a vocation in painting. She poured the same love and good feelings into her art that she had had for Lionel and, consequently, has sold many of her paintings in exhibitions around the country.

Venus, Goddess of Love

The mount of Venus represents the physical body, through which the sense organs of taste, touch, sight, smell, and hearing function. The senses act as the interface between us and the external world, receiving stimuli that allow us to interact with our environment. However, it is important that we recognize the original purpose for which the body and its senses were intended: that is, to be a vehicle through which

Venus, the goddess of love, represents the physical body through which the actual sense organs of taste, touch, sight, smell, and hearing function.

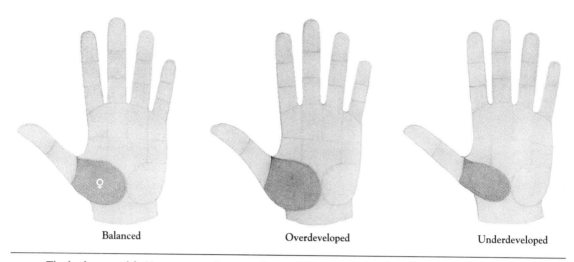

| Balanced | Overdeveloped | Underdeveloped |

The development of the Venus mount indicates to what degree you are relaxed, composed, and free from compulsion.

we evolve, and ultimately, merge with spirit. If we are sidetracked by our senses and become overly self-indulgent, we lose sight of our primary purpose.

An ideal, balanced mount of Venus signifies grace, charm, beauty, and a love of nature. If you have a balanced Venus you are relaxed, composed, and free from compulsions. You move easily in your body and feel at home with yourself. The mount of Venus is ideally somewhat larger than the neighboring mount of Luna. It indicates a loving, compassionate nature that embraces all living things.

Imbalanced Venus

An underdeveloped or overdeveloped Venus mount indicates that you have become preoccupied with the body to the exclusion of spirit. You either indulge in hedonistic pleasure or abstain from the enjoyment of anything physical. In either case, your focus is on the physical as an end in itself rather than as a means through which to manifest your inner spiritual nature.

Overdeveloped Venus

An overdeveloped Venus shows that you may be preoccupied with your body and its comforts, and that preoccupation can result in obsessive-compulsive behavior. Relationships based on physical attraction and a desire for sexual gratification alone may be short-lived, leaving you frustrated, disappointed, and saddened.

By finding alternative areas of interest through which your intense feelings and desires can be redirected, you can moderate your compelling need for sense gratification. If you can do this, your relationships are more likely to become deep and long-lasting, with a balance of spiritual, intellectual, and physical interests.

Miguel: The Simple Life

This successful, world-renowned wildlife photographer channeled his love of beauty into film. After many years of extensive touring, Miguel began to feel that something was missing in his life. He decided to explore his inner world of spirit by becoming a monk, meditating, and living the simple life of a celibate. Although he

Miguel channeled his love of beauty into film.

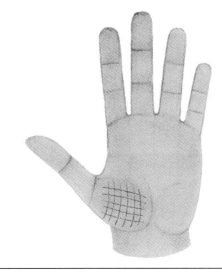

A symmetrical grill on Venus indicates charm and physical attractiveness.

has maintained his resolution, his mount of Venus, the goddess of love, is so highly developed that he continues to attract beautiful women.

UNDERDEVELOPED VENUS

A weak or underdeveloped Venus may be the result of having this mount overdeveloped at one time in the past. Due to past excess, you may now have a weakened nervous system. You may also have poor stamina, as your energy has been partially depleted. This can lead to your feeling indifferent, and consequently you may have a disheartened, passive attitude toward relationships. You need to find a goal or cause that can rekindle your passion. If your desire for self-expression is stimulated you can become more actively involved in life.

SYMMETRICAL GRILL ON MOUNT OF VENUS

A symmetrical grill on Venus, whereby both vertical and horizontal lines are equal, indicates charm and physical attractiveness. It points to a

healthy sexual appetite. However, the grill also shows that we have the potential to transcend the merely physical. Our love has a spiritual dimension that can encompass all of humanity.

Venus, the mount of love, is the only place in the hand where a grill formation indicates positive qualities. It is nature's stamp showing that you are ready to attract love.

The vertical lines in this formation parallel the life line, the gauge of your physical constitution; they are indicators of your stamina. You have the energy required to dive deep into love. Horizontal lines show that you have the desire and ability to express your love in a long-term commitment. You need both the vertical and horizontal lines of a balanced grill in order to realize your desire for a profound relationship.

IRREGULARLY FORMED GRILL ON MOUNT OF VENUS

Too many vertical lines in an irregularly formed grill on Venus indicate that you have depth of feeling. You may, however, be inhibited in your

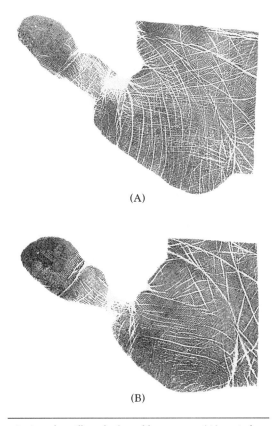

(A)

(B)

An irregular grill can be formed by too many (A) vertical or (B) horizontal lines.

Arlene: Misguided Love

Arlene is physically beautiful. In India, she would be called an *apsara*, or goddess. An irregularly shaped grill on her mount of Venus shows that she has difficulty finding a harmonious outlet for love and is easily discontented. In her search for affection, she is predisposed to indulging in sensuality and extravagance.

Arlene was driven to satisfy her Venusian love of beautiful things. She was, however, unable to support the luxurious lifestyle that reflected her expensive tastes. In her compelling need to satisfy her desires, she even encouraged her son to shoplift. Furthermore, to help finance her expensive tastes, Arlene became entangled with a rich boyfriend who had underworld connections. When he was put in jail, she was tempted to leave him. If she had decided to prove her loyalty and stand by her boyfriend, she might have been able to connect with the positive aspects of Venus and express her affection appropriately.

expression of love as indicated by the absence of equally strong horizontal lines. You need to learn to take risks in love by communicating your feelings to those with whom you would like to develop a relationship.

An irregular grill can also be formed by too many horizontal lines. These lines indicate that you may be quite demonstrative, but lack the stamina and seriousness to sustain your ability to make a commitment to those you love. An overabundance of horizontal lines shows that you have "no brakes." You need to slow down and be more discriminating, instead of leaping into relationships that may cause more conflict than compatibility.

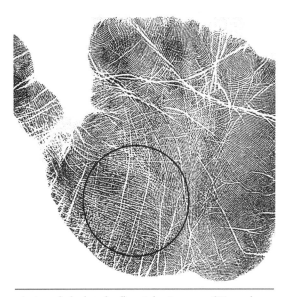

An irregularly shaped grill on Arlene's mount of Venus shows that she has difficulty finding a harmonious outlet for her love.

IRREGULAR CAPILLARY FORMATION ON THE MOUNT OF VENUS

The tiny ridges that constitute the basic skin pattern are known in palmistry as capillaries. An irregular capillary formation on the mount of Venus reflects heightened senses. It indicates a tendency to spend an excessive amount of time and energy gratifying your desire for comfort and pleasure. You may be physically attractive and have a pleasing voice. You may also have an interest in the creative arts. It is important, however, that you channel your love of beauty into some creative and useful form of expression. Otherwise, you may simply overindulge in a lifetime of sensual pleasures.

Steve: Variety Is the Spice of Life

Before Steve was engaged to be married he had led a somewhat bohemian life, which included encounters with numerous women. As his wedding day approached, he questioned whether he would be able to remain faithful to his future wife. Consequently, he visited one of his friends who had been happily married for several years. "How is it possible to love only one person in life when women, for me, are like an orchard of fruit trees," he asked. "How can I settle for one fruit, when they are all so appealing?"

Although the capillary on Steve's mount of Venus highlights his enjoyment of all that is beautiful, he discovered a new source of fulfillment in being married. His two children, both girls, are the joy of his life, and he has devoted himself to nurturing their creative endeavors.

The danger with an unusual capillary formation on Venus is that you may lose sight of the childlike innocence, beauty, and gentle nature indicated by the positive expression of this mount. You need to guard against seeking

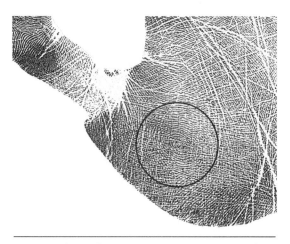

An irregular capillary formation on Venus exaggerates the attributes of this mount.

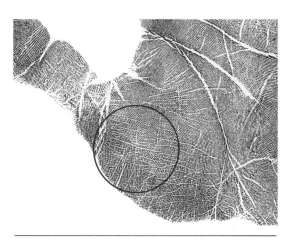

The capillary formation on Steve's mount of Venus highlights his enjoyment of all that is beautiful.

the immediately gratifying experiences that the physical body offers.

Texture

The texture of the hand refers to the fineness or coarseness of the skin capillaries. These may be very close together, forming a fine texture, they may be spaced far apart—a coarse texture—or they may fall somewhere in between these extreme categories, constituting a medium texture. An examination of the texture of the hand yields information concerning the balance of motor and sensory nerves in the body.

FINE TEXTURE

Ridges, or capillaries, that are so finely joined that you need a magnifying glass to distinguish them indicate an inclination toward being overly sensitive. You lack motor strength and basic vitality and, at the same time, exhibit a highly developed sensitivity. You may even be emotionally vulnerable and display a tendency toward indolence.

COARSE TEXTURE

A coarse-textured hand indicates that your motor nerves are strongly developed. Although you may be lacking in sensory refinement, you have vitality, strength, and stamina.

MEDIUM TEXTURE

A medium texture indicates that you possess not only mental refinement, but also the physical strength to express yourself.

Sean and Bev: Opposites Attract

Sean's coarse-textured hand shows that he is not as refined in temperament as Bev, whose hand is more finely textured. Sean, a real estate broker, is vigorous and intense, while Bev is very sensitive. When they got married, Sean provided her with the security and the motivation to do something with her life. With his support, she attended a university and received a degree in psychology.

Sean and Bev complement each other's energies. She encourages him to broaden his horizons, while he provides a haven that grounds her sensitivity.

THE NATURE OF LOVE

Although as souls we all emanate from one source of divine light, each of us has a personal and unique purpose, which we must strive to develop. Unless we do, we cannot find inner peace. We may try to evade this process of self-development by indulging our senses in the physical world of form. The satisfaction gained, however, is temporary, and simply slows down our rate of evolution and the achievement of long-lasting happiness.

Fine

Coarse

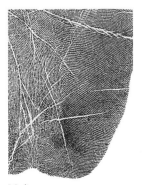
Medium

An examination of the texture of the hand yields information concerning the balance of motor and sensory nerves in the body.

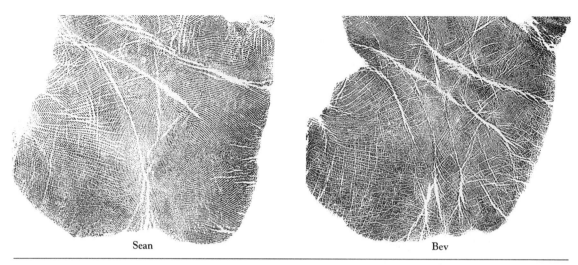

Sean   Bev

Sean and Bev complement each other's energies. She encourages him to broaden his horizons,
while he provides a haven that grounds her sensitivity.

Testing for Resilience

An important test in determining if the mounts are balanced is to check their resilience. When a mount is pressed, it should have some give, and then return quickly to its original shape. A hard mount, when pressed, will be firm and not easily indented by finger pressure. A soft mount is spongy and easily gives in to even slight pressure. The soft mount remains indented for a few moments, slowly returning to its original shape.

HARD MOUNT OF VENUS

A Venus mount that is hard to the touch indicates that you are unresponsive. This can be the result of two things: a hard mount of Venus with refined texture shows a reaction to oversensitivity in which you create a psycho-physiological block; a hard Venus mount with coarse texture is not an indication of sensitivity but of an overly intense, passionate nature—you are so obsessed and wound up inside that you are out of touch with your partner's needs.

A hard mount of Venus with refined texture indicates an extremely sensitive nature. It also indicates that you may have been hurt or extremely disappointed at some point in your past. You feel emotionally vulnerable and, as a result, create a psychological barrier, or armor, that you

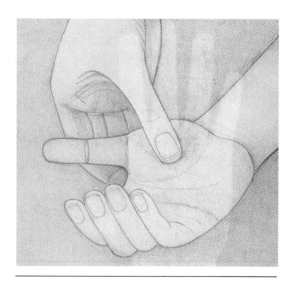

An important test in determining whether the mounts are balanced is to check their resilience.

use to hold people at arm's length. You may be reticent about opening up to others—apprehensive that you may be disappointed and hurt again. People with a hard mount of Venus often develop obsessive and compulsive behavior patterns, becoming rigid and unyielding in temperament.

Although you may feel more secure being insulated from others—safeguarded from hurt—you can become imprisoned. You can prevent yourself from experiencing the richness of life by limiting your interaction with those around you. Deep body massage is beneficial. It allows you to release your unconscious fears so that eventually you can relax and become more trusting.

A hard mount of Venus with coarse texture indicates a pent-up intense, passionate nature. Your sensitivity is overshadowed because you are so compulsive about your own needs and desires that you fail to see what your partner is feeling. In this case, you also need to relax and be more objective, so that your needs are in tune with your partner's.

Cynthia: Obsessive Love

Cynthia, a dynamic, bright, and inquisitive lady in her midfifties, works with mentally challenged young adults. She has pioneered innovative techniques for treating her patients, with which she has had astonishing results. Note her strong head line. Her hard Venus mount reflects her intense, highly charged energy, with which she is able to give a lot of love to the patients under her care. In her personal life, however, the same hard Venus made her compulsive toward Al, whom she felt was, perhaps, her last chance for love. She focused her intensity on developing a relationship with him.

Unfortunately, in her blind enthusiasm, Cynthia neglected to take Al's feelings or needs

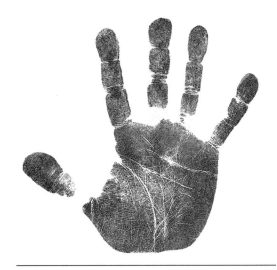

Cynthia's dominant, hard Venus and straight head line indicate her compulsive nature.

into account. Al was having difficulty making a commitment. He had just divorced and was overwhelmed by personal problems. Completely enmeshed in her desire for him, Cynthia was insensitive to his circumstances and called him relentlessly. Their short-lived relationship ended abruptly.

In Cynthia's all-consuming desire to attract Al, she neglected her job, which she later lost.

Cynthia's dominant, hard Venus mount indicates the compulsion she feels to go after what she wants, regardless of the consequences. Her obsessive nature left no room for Al to come to her. For her patients she felt no expectations, and could freely direct all her intense energy toward helping them. In her romantic life, however, Cynthia's definition of love was based on need and expectations rather than on caring and understanding.

SOFT MOUNT OF VENUS

A soft Venus mount indicates that you may have difficulty staying motivated and goal-oriented because you prefer comfort to hard work. You love harmony, but have a tendency to be passive. Although gentle and sensitive, you need to develop more fire and passion. Your sympathetic nature can then be directed toward helping others rather than being used as an excuse for withdrawing from life.

Brian: A Gentle Soul

Brian is kind-hearted, sensitive, and intelligent. He longs to be a successful journalist. The inertia indicated by his soft mount of Venus, however, shows the lack of fire and intensity he requires to be a success. Brian's reticence is also reflected in his personal life. He rarely develops a personal relationship, as pursuit of the person who interests him demands too much energy.

Physical exercise, such as yoga or tai chi, would be beneficial. By developing greater stamina, Brian would be more likely to realize both his career and personal goals.

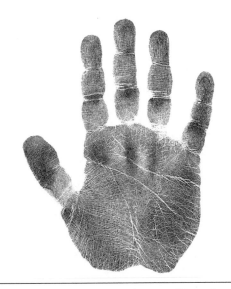

The inertia indicated by Brian's soft mount of Venus shows the lack of fire and intensity he requires to be a success.

Girdle of Venus

The girdle of Venus ideally originates between the fingers of Jupiter and Saturn. It then continues in a crescentlike curve that travels across the mounts on the sattwic world of the palm, terminating between the fingers of Sun and Mercury.

The mount of Venus, located in the tamasic world, represents the physical expression of love. A girdle of Venus located in the sattwic world, however, shows the desire to redirect passion away from the strictly physical toward more sublime areas of creativity. Its ideal formation joins both the inner and outer worlds of the hand, showing the ability to channel your inner passion outwardly through art or music. You are highly sensitive and empathetic toward others.

The ideal girdle of Venus is not commonly found. It represents the ability and discipline to transform personal experience into universal expression. The artist's passionate love for art is unconditional, and through its excellence inspires others. One who has the girdle of Venus is able to open others' hearts to universal beauty and truth.

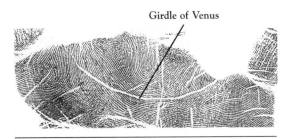

The girdle of Venus reflects artistic sensitivity.

Sister Madeleine: Loving the Enemy

Sister Madeleine witnessed and endured atrocities in a Pacific prisoner-of-war camp during World War II, yet she continued her work in

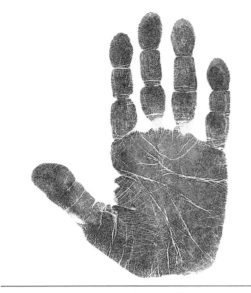

Sister Madeleine's well-formed girdle of Venus gives her an extraordinary quality of forgiveness.

that same region after the war. Now well into her seventies, she still strives for international harmony and cooperation, without a trace of bitterness. Note the well-formed girdle of Venus, which gives her this extraordinary quality of forgiveness.

BROKEN GIRDLE OF VENUS

A broken girdle of Venus, more commonly found, indicates that if the creative force is not channeled properly, escapism and emotionalism

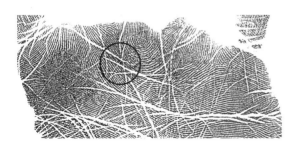

A broken girdle of Venus indicates unchanneled sensitivity, which may result in unpredictable emotions and escapism.

can override the psyche, deflecting creativity.

Before being drawn impulsively toward forming a lifetime commitment to a companion, you should evaluate your motivation for entering into the relationship. Situations that appear attractive at first may be short-lived. Before getting too deeply involved, you need to examine the depth and continuity of your feelings for your partner.

Alexander: An Empath

Alexander is a talented artist working for a major film studio. One day on the bus coming home from work a lady sitting beside him got her hand caught in the window. Alexander felt the intensity of her pain and jumped up to help her. A short time later, he came to, and discovered that he had been carried off the bus as he had fainted. The presence of a girdle of Venus

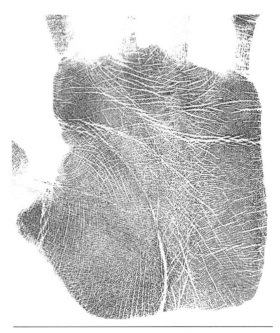

The presence of breaks in Alexander's girdle of Venus indicates that he is prone to be overwhelmed by his emotions.

shows that he has tremendous empathy; however, the breaks indicate that he is prone to being overwhelmed by his emotions.

Island in Girdle of Venus

An island in the girdle of Venus indicates an inability to perceive the intentions of others. You may feel disillusioned, disappointed, or betrayed; hence your sensitivity is directed toward your own suffering. You are unable to transcend personal pain in order to become sufficiently objective about whom you attract in your relationships.

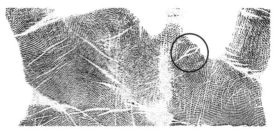

Before

After

The emotional healing that Kurt experienced after much disappointment and unhappiness in his relationship is shown by the disappearance of the island in the second hand print.

The "after" handprint shows that the island in the girdle has dissolved. Kurt attributes this to intense therapy work. Additionally, his mother had a stroke, losing the power of speech that she had used to belittle him as a child. He became her caregiver, which offered him the chance to tell her how he was feeling, and she became open enough to listen. The situation resulted in an emotional healing for both of them.

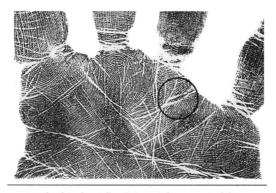

An island in the girdle of Venus indicates an inability to exercise discrimination in relationships.

Kurt: An Emotional Healing

The island on Kurt's girdle of Venus in the "before" print shows that he has experienced disappointment and unhappiness in his relationships. The presence of the girdle itself reveals Kurt's sensitivity and creativity, which are evident in his poetry. His writing became a great outlet for the sadness he felt stemming from his mother's rejection of him as a child. His unresolved grief and feelings of insecurity led to a pattern of attracting women who ended up rejecting him.

Via Lascivia

The via lascivia reflects the opposite characteristics of those represented by the girdle of Venus. The girdle of Venus, located in the sattwic zone of the hand, shows that you are able to free yourself from the limitations of the purely physical. The via lascivia, located in the tamasic zone of the hand, indicates that you are

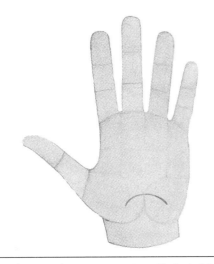

The via lascivia indicates preoccupation with physical desires.

Mars, the god of war, represents our active or reactive response to the events in our lives.

preoccupied by physical desires. Unless you learn to look beyond the need for immediate sensory gratification, you will be unable to develop profound, loving relationships.

Mars, God of Destruction and Rejuvenation

Mythologically, Mars is considered to be the planet of war and destruction. It is often referred to as malefic. However, the purpose of Mars the warrior is to protect the weak, provide stability, and maintain peace. Ideally, the presence alone of the warrior accomplishes these, and force is used only as a last resort. The stronger the warrior, the less force is required. Mars, then, can be our greatest ally when its energy is channeled properly.

The mounts of Mars positive (+) and Mars negative (−), which together make up the Mars galaxy, reflect the degree of energy and stamina operating in your life. Ideally, Mars positive, which represents mental strength, indicates your resolution to be steadfast, calm, and productive. Mars negative, which represents physical strength, reflects your ability to implement these resolutions in everyday life.

Most people have a balanced Mars positive; however, a balanced Mars negative is less frequently found. It is easier to resolve to be calm in the face of opposition than to refuse to react negatively when provoked.

OVERDEVELOPED MARS POSITIVE

An overdeveloped Mars positive indicates a tendency to be self-centered. You place your own needs and desires first, creating an environment hostile to peace. You may tend to be possessive, overly assertive, and stubborn. Your compulsive desire to get what you want poses a threat to your relationships. You need to find an appropriate, constructive outlet for your energy.

By learning to harmonize your partner's wishes, dreams, and ambitions with your own, you can minimize the detrimental effects of an overdeveloped Mars positive.

UNDERDEVELOPED MARS POSITIVE

An underdeveloped Mars positive indicates listlessness and timidity. You may lack the mental energy to cope with stressful situations and tend to give up easily. You are more likely to seek a relationship in which you feel sheltered. You can develop your confidence by setting easily attainable goals; with each success your ability to persevere can grow.

OVERDEVELOPED MARS NEGATIVE

An overdeveloped Mars negative reflects a nature that is prone to overreacting. You may have a tendency to be sarcastic and aggressive, and can easily intimidate your partner. You need to practice "counting to ten" before you respond to a situation that stirs your emotions. By cultivating respect for others and realizing that aggressive behavior does not achieve positive results, you can learn to acquire a sense of calm.

UNDERDEVELOPED MARS NEGATIVE

An underdeveloped Mars negative suggests vulnerability, indifference, and poor physical stamina. A repressed attitude and pessimistic outlook on life make it difficult to attract a happy relationship. You have a tendency toward self-pity and seek reassurance from others. You need to make a conscious effort to determine the cause of your lack of stamina. As well as taking steps to adopt a healthy physical regimen, you should cultivate a positive environment in order to build self-reliance. You should attempt simple tasks until your nervous system gains proper strength. Constructive role models can encourage you to become more independent and assertive.

Paula and Donald: Complementary Opposites

Paula is brilliant, as indicated by her strong intense head line. However, she is missing the stamina necessary to channel the intense flow of her ideas, which is shown by her underdeveloped mounts of Mars positive and negative. On

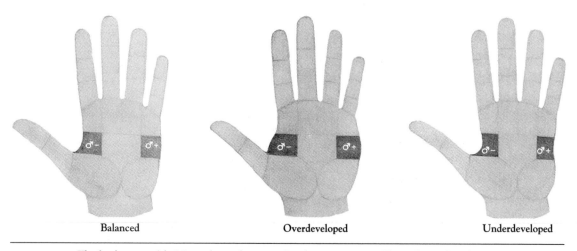

Balanced   Overdeveloped   Underdeveloped

The development of the Mars galaxy indicates to what degree you are steadfast, calm, and productive.

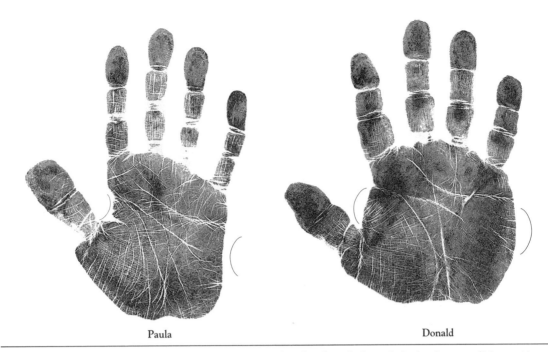

Paula   Donald

Paula is missing the stamina necessary to channel the intense flow of her ideas shown by her underdeveloped mounts of Mars positive and negative. Donald's well-developed mounts show that he is more confident and extroverted, thus able to help calm Paula's jangled nerves.

the contrary, Donald has both these mounts well-developed. He is more confident, extroverted, and has helped calm her jangled nerves. In this case Paula has thrived with his support and is now a confident executive in a bank.

Andrea: It Takes Strength to Love

Andrea, who was adopted, dreamed for years of finding her biological father. Now a successful actress, she is finally reunited with him after months of research. Over a short period of time, however, Andrea became concerned about the lavish attention she was receiving from him. She felt threatened that her personal lifestyle would be upset.

Her underdeveloped Mars negative indicates her lack of endurance and stamina. Andrea's energy had been consumed dreaming of a reunion that she was incapable of managing when it became a reality.

It takes strength to love. Had Andrea recognized her inherent weaknesses earlier, and taken steps to strengthen herself in preparation for the reunion, she would have been more able to enjoy the relationship.

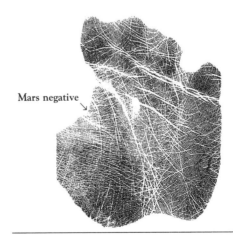

Mars negative

Andrea's underdeveloped Mars negative indicates her lack of endurance and stamina.

BALL ON MOUNT OF MARS NEGATIVE

Found in most hands, a ball on the mount of Mars negative indicates that you have difficulty letting go of hurt and misunderstandings. You have a tendency to analyze any response that you perceive as negative. You may nurse apparent injury rather than letting it go. Learning how not to hold on to negativity is a step on the path toward loving unconditionally.

Before

A ball on the mount of Mars negative indicates difficulty in letting go of hurt and misunderstandings.

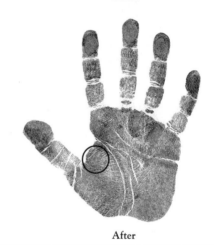

After

Anita's first print reveals a ball on Mars negative. In her second hand print, the ball is reduced.

Anita: Forgiveness and Self-Acceptance

The "before" print reveals a ball on Mars negative. Anita had been physically, emotionally, and sexually abused by her father. Her first husband was an alcoholic who repeated the same pattern of abuse. Many years later she remarried, only to experience more physical and emotional torment. Finally she recognized that she had problems and began therapy in order to break this destructive pattern. She learned to appreciate herself as no one else had been able

to do. In her "after" hand print, her progress is reflected in the reduction in size of the ball on Mars negative.

STAR ON MOUNT OF MARS NEGATIVE

A star on Mars negative suggests a hot temper. You may be likely to explode with anger when your expectations are not met. You need to become more forgiving and learn how to restrain your inappropriate reactions to situations that hurt or disappoint you.

A star on Mars negative suggests a hot temper.

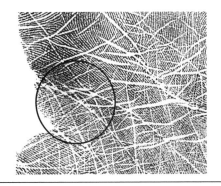

Interference lines on the mount of Mars negative indicate unresolved incidents from the past.

INTERFERENCE LINES ON MOUNT OF MARS NEGATIVE

Horizontal lines crossing the mount indicate a disturbance of energy stemming from some unresolved incident in your past. You need to make a conscious effort to react to the situation objectively. You must guard against reacting according to early negative conditioning.

CAPILLARY PATTERN ON MOUNT OF MARS NEGATIVE

A capillary pattern on Mars negative shows that you have a fiery nature that is easily aggravated. You need to seek out a calm, peaceful environment and find appropriate outlets for channeling your energy.

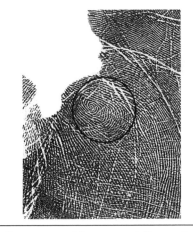

A capillary pattern on Mars negative indicates a fiery nature.

Love Signs on Mars Positive

POORVA PUNYA

Poorva Punya, a Hindi term, translates as "good fortune earned as a result of meritorious past-life deeds." When it is present, it reflects that you are gifted with rare charm to attract someone of

Poorva Punya

The Poorva Punya line is an indication of good fortune.

the opposite sex with whom you have a common goal. Its origin on the mount of Mars positive (past-life memories) indicates that you are intuitively aware of goals set in the past that you are now in the process of completing. The progress of the Poorva Punya line past the heart line and on to the mount of Sun (the mount of success) indicates the potential to realize these goals.

The personal magnetism and charm resulting from the development of this line also indicate your attractiveness to the opposite sex. You can develop relationships with those who come into your life from previous lifetimes so that, together, you can realize a common goal. The Poorva Punya also indicates your commitment and loyalty to your partner.

Love Signs on Mars Negative

MARS ASSISTANT LINE

The Mars assistant line originates on or near the mount of Mars negative. It then curves down onto the mount of Venus, paralleling the life line. Ideally, it should not touch the life line or travel too close to it.

The Mars assistant line acts as a secondary life line. It shows that you have reserves of energy and stamina to help support your activities. The formation of this line also reflects your attitude toward life and the kinds of relationships that you attract.

A well-formed Mars assistant line shows that your attitude toward life is open, self-renewing, and energetic. The people in your life generally help you and are a source of motivation and inspiration. Consequently, the Mars assistant line indicates that you can attract and develop positive and supportive relationships.

IRREGULARITIES IN MARS ASSISTANT LINE

Irregularities in the Mars assistant line show that your attitude toward life is not well balanced. You tend to attract individuals with whose attitudes you are in conflict. If you can learn from these encounters, they may challenge you to restructure your ways of thinking—

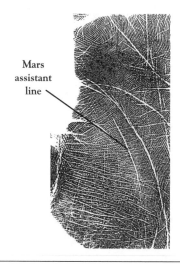

Mars
assistant
line

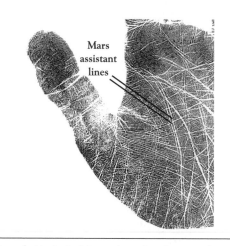

Mars
assistant
lines

The Mars assistant line shows an ability to attract and develop positive and supportive relationships.

Irregularities in the Mars assistant line show a tendency to attract individuals with conflicting attitudes.

to become more hopeful, open, and positive in your personal view of life.

MARS ASSISTANT LINE ORIGINATING FROM LIFE LINE

A Mars assistant line originating from the life line indicates that someone in your life is exhausting your energy and stamina rather than helping you to renew them. Perhaps you have depended too much on others, failing to develop your own reserves of energy. As a result, you can feel trapped in circumstances in which you allow others to dominate you. In your desire for security, you forfeit your self-reliance and diminish personal motivation. You must learn to stand on your own—appreciating, yet not dependent on, what others have to offer.

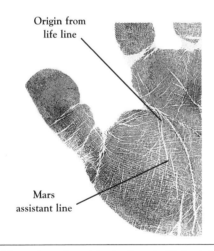

Origin from life line

Mars assistant line

A Mars assistant line originating from the life line indicates that your energy is being exhausted.

MARS ASSISTANT LINE TERMINATING ON LIFE LINE

A termination of the Mars assistant line on the life line indicates that you have temporarily lost

A termination of the Mars assistant line on the life line indicates a loss of motivation.

the motivating force that had previously sustained you.

A conflict in a relationship may drain your energies. Your potential to continue a motivated and structured lifestyle is indicated by a healthy continuation of the life line.

Union Line: Degree of Commitment in Love

MOUNT OF MERCURY

The union line is found on the mount of Mercury. In classical Indian palmistry, the Mercury mount and finger are referred to as the domain of Buddha. This area reflects your degree of attachment to the material world. It also reveals to what degree you have profound, unshakable inner peace. An ideal Mercury shows that your nature is like the Buddha, this mount's namesake, who left the wealth and social standing he was born to so that he could develop inner liberation.

Mercury is referred to as the Buddha, the Enlightened One.

THE UNION LINE AS A REFLECTION OF COMMITMENT

As with all the lines and signs of the hand, union lines reflect potential circumstances. For example, a nun may have a profound union line, whereas a married man may have no union line at all. The nun has a deep desire for a profound relationship that finds expression in her marriage with God. The husband may have married to satisfy the expectations of his family.

Union lines represent profound relationships.

IDEAL UNION LINE

Ideally, there should be one straight horizontal union line. It should be long, deep, and without any interferences throughout its length. This formation indicates your desire for a profound, loving relationship.

The number of union lines and their formation show your attitude toward initiating, developing, and sustaining a partnership.

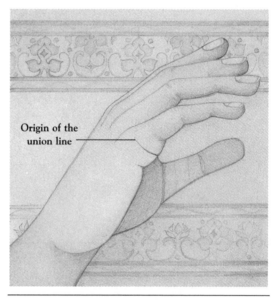

The origin of the union line can sometimes be traced to the back of the hand.

Karmic Relationships

Union lines that extend to the back of the hand represent profound karmic relationships that you started in past lives. They indicate your potential ability to renew these associations and to continue your evolution through them. The first time you meet your partner, there is an instant feeling of recognition and familiarity.

DETERMINING THE LIKELIHOOD OF MARRIAGE

To determine the likelihood of marriage, it is always important to check the hands of both partners. You can have a deep desire for someone; however, unless he or she has a union line at the same time in the hand with the same intensity, it may be difficult to develop a long-lasting relationship.

You must also verify your own depth of feeling. The union line may be present in the active hand but not in the inactive one at the same time. Or it may be present in the inactive hand as a subconscious desire that has not yet surfaced as a line in the active hand.

SINGLE UNION LINE

A single union line shows that you are serious and exclusive in a relationship. You are committed and loyal to your partner.

A single union line shows an ability to be exclusive in a relationship.

Delia and Gerald: A Fan Finds Her Idol

Delia and Gerald each have a single union line. She was thirty-two and he was thirty-eight when they first met. These ages coincide with the timing on their individual union lines, and reflect

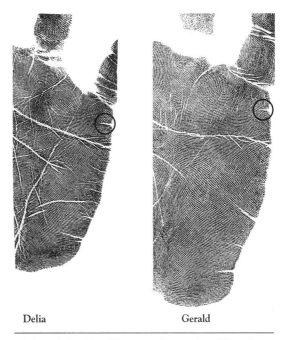

Delia	Gerald

Delia and Gerald each have a single union line. This reflects their mutual attraction.

the sudden attraction they had for each other. In addition, both have union lines that extend to the back of their hands. They felt at home with each other as soon as they were introduced. Delia began taking piano lessons with Gerald, and both felt that somewhere they had done this before. She became his most ardent fan, accompanying him on concert tours. They eventually married.

MANY UNION LINES

It is not uncommon to find four or five union lines on the mount of Mercury. An appreciable distance between each line (A) indicates that you may be involved in several relationships during the course of your life—each one playing a significant role in your evolution.

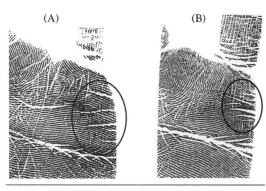

(A)   (B)

The number of union lines and the spacing between them indicate attitudes toward forming a relationship.

However, many union lines tightly clustered together (B) indicate that you enjoy having many partners but have difficulty making a commitment to one person.

Harry: Enough Is Not Enough

Time is of no concern to Harry, who is young, mobile, and independently rich. His many union lines, combined with his hedonistic lifestyle, have led Harry from one romance to another. His numerous union lines indicate his need for stimulation and excitement. It is important that he learn to redefine his concept of love, otherwise, he may never be able to actually experience it.

LONG UNION LINE

A long union line is one that extends past the Mercury mount and onto the mount of Sun. It indicates your potential to attract a partner who may be prominent and recognized by society. This line terminating on the Sun, your public magnetism, shows that you may also receive public exposure through this association. The desire for such a distinctive relationship, however, may be based on your need for prestige and respect.

A long union line present in both your active and inactive hands is significant. It shows that you not only have the magnetism to attract a high profile relationship, but that you have the stamina and endurance to sustain and enjoy a long-lasting relationship.

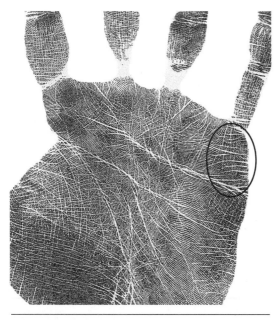

Harry's numerous union lines indicate his need for stimulus and excitement.

A long union line.

FLOATING UNION LINE

A union line that appears to float in the middle of the Mercury mount indicates that you may form a relationship with someone with whom you have no karmic ties. This line shows a conscious desire to create a new karmic bond.

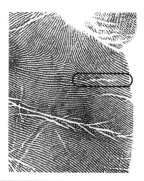

A floating union line.

CLOSE AND PARALLEL UNION LINES

Parallel union lines that are too close together indicate that you may have difficulty making a commitment in a relationship. Although you are with your partner, you may be dreaming of someone else. Perhaps you are disappointed that your partner does not live up to your idealized vision of the perfect soul mate. In your discontent, you can become ambivalent and undermine the relationship.

None of us is perfect. However, we can often become our best self through the process of committing to a relationship. The joy that comes from the bond of love brings satisfaction and contentment.

UPWARD-TURNING UNION LINE

An upward-turning union line indicates ambiguity about having a partner. The presence of this line indicates your desire for a relationship. Its upwardly angled termination, however, suggests your desire to be independent and free from restrictions.

We learn to grow, evolve, and ultimately become happier through the structures we create in life—one of them being our intimate relationships. This understood, you may be able to resolve the dilemma indicated by this formation. Over time, you may come to appreciate that the potential benefits of having a loving relationship outweigh your desire to be free and independent.

Parallel union lines.

An upward-turning union line indicates ambiguity about having a partner.

DOWNWARD-TURNING UNION LINE

A union line that turns downward toward Mars positive shows that, in relationships, you express the aggressive and powerful energy indicated by Mars. Ideally, if you have this line, you should find a partner with the same downward-turning union line. Otherwise, you can overwhelm your partner with your possessive, forceful, and demanding nature. In India, this formation is referred to as *mangli*. There, where arranged marriages are common, parents marrying a son or daughter with this formation will seek a mangli partner for them.

It is important for you to channel your intensity through physical work, intellectual pursuits, or spiritual practice, such as meditation. In its extreme form, a mangli line can indicate a loss of objectivity and common sense due to an abnormally possessive nature.

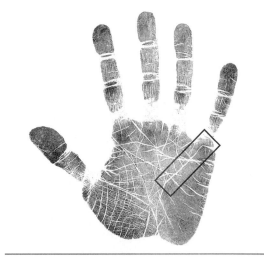

Norman has an extremely mangli union line that descends deep into his hand.

A mangli (downward-turning) union line indicates that you can overwhelm your partner.

Norman: Trouble Letting Go

Norman has an extremely mangli union line. It descends deep into his hand, joining the Mercury line. Norman was overwhelmed by the death of his fiancée, Marie, who died just two weeks before their wedding date. Unable to accept his loss, Norman actually believed that she was still living with him in their apartment. After months of

therapy, however, he regained his objective grasp of reality and was finally able to let Marie go.

Marge: Smoothing Out Difficulties

Marge went through a period of major life changes. At the time of the "before" print her

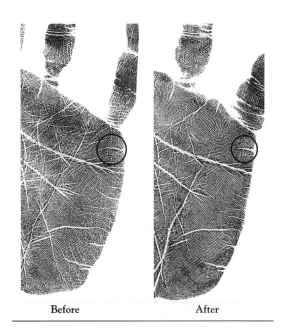

| Before | After |

Marge's positive change in attitude toward her relationship is reflected in her union line that changed from mangli (before) to straight (after).

mother had just recently died, she had ended a ten-year relationship, and she had recently moved to another city to begin a new job. Under these trying circumstances she had difficulty maintaining her composure, which carried over into her new relationship. During this period in her life, Marge's union line was mangli.

Richard has a straight union line. When he and Marge met, they immediately fell in love. After a few weeks together, however, the conflicts began. Over the following two years Marge learned to readjust her entire attitude toward life. She was courageous and open to change and, with Richard's help, she became sweeter in temperament and more easygoing. This transformation is reflected in her union line, which changed from mangli to straight. The fact that now they both have straight union lines indicates a greater potential for Marge and Richard to lead a happy and harmonious life together.

ISLANDED UNION LINE

An islanded union line indicates that you may have some unresolved inner conflict relating directly to your partner. An island in the middle of the line shows that the difficulties you experience, however challenging, may be overcome. This is confirmed when the line continues strongly after the island formation. Ideally, the disap-

pearance of an island indicates that, over a period of time, you have resolved your negative feelings. An island located at the end of the union line is more serious; it indicates an inability to come to terms with how you feel in your present relationship. Cultivating a positive and less judgmental attitude allows you to break free of the negative emotions that may end the relationship prematurely.

VERTICAL LINES CROSSING UNION LINE

Vertical lines crossing the union line indicate that external circumstances can affect the stability of your relationship. You choose your partner; however, you do not select the family, friends, and circumstances that accompany him or her. For example, your father-in-law may be reluctant to get to know you. Perhaps he still remembers his son- or daughter-in-law, whom he really loved, from a previous marriage. Although it may be a struggle to be fully accepted into the family, you should remain kind and loving. Regardless of how challenging the situation may be, you give others the freedom to be as they are by keeping an open heart.

Vertical lines crossing the union line indicate that external circumstances can negatively affect relationships.

FORK AT ORIGIN OF UNION LINE

A fork at the origin of the union line shows that you have a dissimilar cultural, social, or religious

An islanded union line indicates conflict in a relationship.

background to your partner. At the beginning of your relationship, these differences may generate some conflict or misunderstanding. The union line that continues after the fork, however, indicates that you can resolve whatever problems stem from your contrasting viewpoints. Ideally, the disappearance of the fork, over time, suggests that all traces of earlier misunderstanding have disappeared.

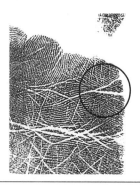

A fork at the origin of the union line.

FORK AT TERMINATION OF UNION LINE

Similar to the forked origin of the union line, a fork at its termination indicates that there are cultural, religious, and/or social differences between you and your partner. Although these differences appear to be insignificant initially, as time passes, you may find you have a variety of important issues that need to be addressed. For example, you may ask, "In what religion will our children be raised?" or "Should we celebrate Christmas or Hanukkah—or both?"

The forked termination shows that unless you learn to accommodate each other's differences, you may drift apart from one another.

FORK WITH TONGUE AT END OF UNION LINE

A union line whose termination is forked and has a "tongue" indicates that there are significant cultural, religious, and social differences between you and your partner. The addition of the tongue in the fork reflects your inability to reconcile your differences. You may end up driving a wedge between yourself and your partner. The end result can be the dissolution of the relationship.

You should probably question why you are motivated to seek out someone whose background is so different from yours. You might reply that you are expressing universal love. However, rather than truly being one with all mankind, you may simply be fascinated by differences.

The forked termination shows that unless you learn to accommodate each other's differences, your relationship may end.

A forked union line with a tongue indicates that you may attract someone whose background and attitudes conflict with yours.

ABSENCE OF UNION LINE

Whereas a union line indicates a conscious awareness of the dynamics of a relationship, the absence of a union line suggests that you are not fully conscious of the implications of forming a serious commitment with someone. Perhaps you have not yet recognized the importance of developing a committed and loving relationship. You may seek out partners who can satisfy your needs and desires physically and emotionally, but the depth of your relationships is secondary in importance.

The absence of a union line indicates the importance of developing a committed relationship.

GROWING A UNION LINE

By making a conscious effort to be more tolerant and forgiving, and by learning to be sensitive to the needs of your partner—sometimes at the expense of your own desires, you can develop a successful relationship. As a result, your union line may begin to grow.

Lorne: Learning to Make a Commitment

Lorne and Vanessa are happily married. At the beginning of their relationship, Vanessa was enthusiastic and wanted an early marriage. Although Lorne was a free spirit, he finally agreed. At the time of their wedding, Lorne had

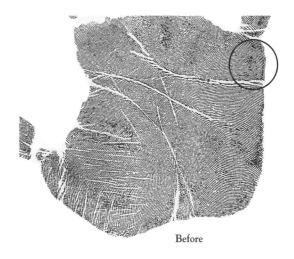

Before

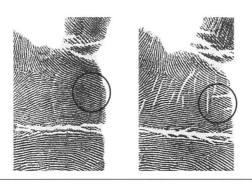

Along with learning to become more tolerant and forgiving, the union line may begin to grow.

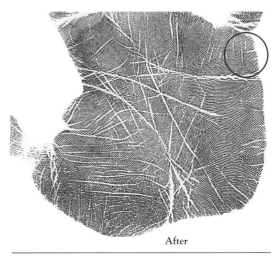

After

Within a period of six months, Lorne's union line developed.

no union line and felt no necessity to make a commitment to her. At first, Vanessa seemed only to curb his carefree lifestyle. Six months later, however, he began to realize the importance of a serious and committed relationship. Subsequently, his hand prints indicated the appearance of a union line. They had several children and together opened a clothing boutique, which continues to flourish.

WISDOM MARKINGS: DEVELOPING SENSITIVITY FOR OTHERS

A number of markings—for example, crosses, squares, tridents, and stars—may indicate positive qualities, depending on their locations.

We refer to these auspicious signs as wisdom markings. They show that you have developed greater maturity and reliability and are becoming more consciously aware of others. These positive markings indicate that you are able to express the ideal qualities associated with the mount on which they are found. Since wisdom markings reflect a conscious degree of self-understanding, they represent the potential ability to strengthen relationships.

Square on Mount of Jupiter

A square on Jupiter reflects your attraction to universal ideas. It suggests that you are drawn to explore the four corners of the world, either mentally or physically. You may attract relationships with those from other nationalities.

Jupiter is the mount that signifies your sense of identity and purpose in life. It stands for *guru*, which translates as "dispeller of darkness." The square indicates an expanded awareness. You perceive your goals as intertwined with all individuals, races, and creeds. You recognize that humanity is, in essence, all made up of the same energy, and your ambition is to support the welfare of your neighbors. You can be a world teacher bringing this understanding to others—often through writing.

If your partner does not share your universal

1. Star on Jupiter
2. Cross on Jupiter
3. Square on Jupiter
4. Ring of Solomon
5. Truth line
6. Healing Stigmata

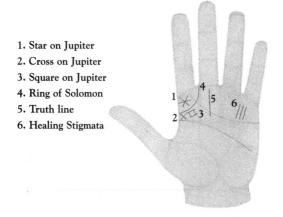

Wisdom markings show an increase in your ability to empathize.

A square on Jupiter suggests a tendency to attract relationships with those of other nationalities.

spirit and flexibility of attitude, you may feel alone. Therefore, you are inclined to seek a relationship with a like-minded partner.

Cross on Mount of Jupiter

A cross on Jupiter shows that you are consciously seeking your identity and direction in life. There is an old saying, "When the student is ready, the teacher appears." The energy you generate in the process of self-discovery can attract a partner, teacher, or friend who helps you discover more about yourself. You thereby realize your potential.

This sign indicates an outstanding magnetic personality. You have an intense fascination for the opposite sex. Fortunately, this attraction is based on your desire for a meaningful relationship.

A cross on Jupiter indicates an outstanding magnetic personality.

Ellen: A Student in Search of a Teacher

Ellen has a beautiful cross on her Jupiter mount. Several months before this print was taken, she had been voraciously reading books on metaphysics, philosophy, and psychology. She felt the need to find someone who could help her incorporate her new understanding into her life. One day, a good friend told her about his experience with a palmist who had been invaluable

The cross on Ellen's Jupiter mount indicates her potential to attract good friends and teachers.

in helping her to understand herself better. Consequently, Ellen went to see the palmist and immediately recognized that he was the person she had been searching for. Together they established a school in palmistry incorporating the healing techniques of yoga and meditation.

Star on Mount of Jupiter

A star on Jupiter indicates that you can have outstanding success. If the focus of your ambitions is material or social, you are able to realize these ambitions. If you are spiritually inclined, the star shows that you can be successful in visualizing the spiritual light—sometimes referred to as the third eye in your forehead.

Jupiter stands for the mind and your degree of self-awareness. Your sense of individuality enables you to learn your karmic lessons in life. These lessons most often deal with relationships, especially your ability to love those close to you. As you learn to unconditionally extend

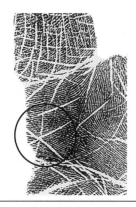

A star on Jupiter indicates that you can accomplish your goals.

yourself toward others, you begin to dissolve the illusory barriers that seem to separate you from others. This process can take lifetimes, or it can happen spontaneously.

For example, those who have had a near-death experience describe going toward a brilliant white light that filled them with an incredible feeling of love. Once revived, they discover new meaning in life. They were freed from the fears and concerns that had troubled them previously, transformed by an absolute feeling of peace and love.

However, you do not have to experience near death, or several more lifetimes, to realize the spirit within. A star on Jupiter indicates that you have already learned to focus your mind and can accomplish whatever goals you set for yourself. By making a dedicated effort to focus on spiritual concerns, you can go beyond the limitations and separating nature of your ego to achieve a higher level of consciousness. Sattwic techniques such as mantra and meditation can help you to recognize an absolute connection with all humankind. As a result, it becomes natural for you to see the success of others as your own success.

Others can benefit from your greater understanding and realization. Your connection with spirit creates a magnetism that can attract a worldwide audience. You touch the hearts of all those with whom you come in contact. In spirit, you may finally develop the ultimate relationship in which you become one with everything.

Brother Dennis: A Playboy Serves Humanity

Brother Dennis has a well-formed star on his mount of Jupiter. Before he joined a monastic order, he had lived a fast-paced life as a freelance engineering consultant. The focus of his energy was directed toward physical pleasure and the acquisition of material things. Although very successful, he began to feel lost and eventually came to a crossroads in his life. A friend gave him a copy of Paramahansa Yogananda's *Autobiography of a Yogi*. After reading the book, he knew he had found the key that would turn his life around. He started meditating and, finally, joined a monastic order. Brother Dennis was able to rechannel his passionate energy—shown by the overdeveloped Venus mount—into an

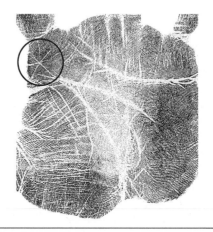

Brother Dennis was successful in channeling his ambitions toward a spiritual life.

equally intense devotion to share divine love as a missionary monk.

Ring of Solomon on Mount of Jupiter

An ideal ring of Solomon circles the mount of Jupiter. This sign indicates your ability to go beyond personal concerns. You are sensitive to social issues, you have the wisdom to perceive the problems of the human condition, and you are committed to the welfare of others. Your intuitive understanding of human psychology serves you well in all your relationships.

A ring of Solomon shows intuitive understanding of human psychology.

Apex on Mount of Jupiter

An ideal apex on Jupiter is centrally located on the mount. It indicates that you are able to realize your own ambitions while maintaining respect for the goals of others. You are charming and magnetic, and have a tendency to attract good luck.

An apex on the inside world of the mount—toward the thumb—shows that you are ambi-

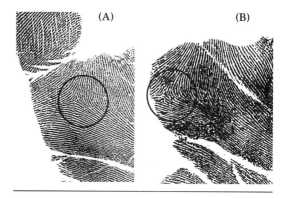

(A) Ideal apex on Jupiter. (B) Apex toward thumb.

tious and self-centered. Your preoccupation with achieving your goals may cause you to disregard the needs of those close to you. You should make an effort to become more sensitive to the feelings of others.

Truth Line on Mount of Saturn

The truth line, a vertical line found on the mount of Saturn, shows that you have a receptivity to others' points of view. You are a good listener and are willing to accept criticism. You

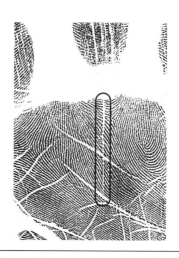

The truth line shows a receptivity to others.

see beyond the observable reality and have an intuitive sense of the metaphysical universe. For this reason, the truth line is often referred to as the love-of-God line.

Healing Stigmata on Mount of Mercury

Ideally, the healing stigmata consist of three small vertical lines on the mount of Mercury. They indicate that you find great pleasure in giving comfort—physical, emotional, mental, and spiritual. For that reason, they are often found on the hands of those in the healing professions. You often have an intuitive sense of the appropriate thing to say or do to alleviate suffering or bring joy.

The healing stigmata indicate that you find great pleasure in giving comfort.

THE FINGERS: OUR CONSCIOUS EXPRESSION

The fingers show an ability to communicate the characteristics of the mounts. The length of your fingers is an indicator of the time it takes

The fingers show an ability to communicate the characteristics of the mounts.

you to respond—both in exhibiting your true feelings and in reacting to what goes on around you.

DETERMINING LENGTH OF FINGERS

A basic rule for determining if your fingers are long or short is to compare two measurements—the width of the hand between Mars positive and Mars negative (Mars galaxy) and the length of the Saturn finger. The Mars galaxy relates to your ability to act, while the Saturn finger relates to the quality of your thinking. If the length of the Saturn finger is greater than the Mars galaxy, you have long fingers. If the reverse is true, you have short fingers. If both measurements are equal, your actions are balanced by discriminating thought.

LONG FINGERS

When the length of the Saturn finger is greater than the width of the Mars galaxy, your thinking takes precedence over your actions. Long fingers indicate that you are deliberate and reflective. You tend not to be spontaneous; you may find it difficult to make quick decisions and act upon them. Although we should all "look before we leap," you may sometimes lose opportunities if you spend too much time weighing alternatives and their possible implications.

SHORT FINGERS

If the width of your Mars galaxy is greater than the length of your Saturn finger, your actions override your thinking. Short fingers indicate that you can be impulsive and impatient. Unless you take time to think through the implications of your actions, you may end up spending even more time undoing your mistakes. In your enthusiasm and spontaneity, you may speak or act inappropriately. As a result, you may unknowingly hurt the feelings of others.

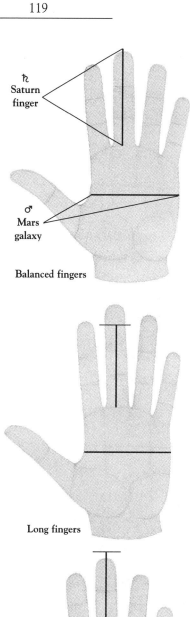

ℏ
**Saturn
finger**

♂
**Mars
galaxy**

Balanced fingers

Long fingers

Short fingers

Determining the length of the fingers.

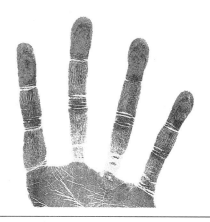

Long fingers indicate a tendency to be deliberate and reflective.

Short fingers indicate a tendency to be impulsive and impatient.

OPPOSITES ATTRACT

Opposites often attract each other and the differences you bring to a relationship can be vitalizing and complementary. However, the reverse may be true and the differences can be devastating. It may be that you initially find your partner's differences appealing, yet, after a period of time, they become annoying. The friction created as a result of your new and demanding dynamic may provide an opportunity to grow. However, the challenge may prove painful and difficult. You may reject the chance to improve yourself through the relationship and instead look to greener pastures.

By working with your partner's differences, you can learn to override your limited and overly structured way of thinking. You can then learn to be tolerant of others and to accommodate their alternative modes of expression and behavior. One such case of opposites attracting is the following couple, one with long fingers and the other with short fingers.

Susan and Andrew: Vive la Différence

Andrew's short fingers are in sharp contrast to the long fingers of his wife, Susan. She was attracted by his refreshing, enthusiastic, and unconstrained personality. He found her quiet, mysterious, and thoughtful temperament particularly appealing and a respite from his hectic lifestyle. After they had been married a few months, however, their differences began annoying each other. For example, they both enjoyed going to films, but they always missed the first scenes of the movie. Andrew would wait in the car for forty-five minutes, restless and fuming, while Susan was still in the bathroom fastidiously flossing her teeth, unaware of his agitation.

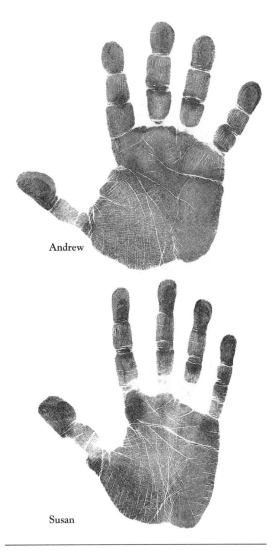

Andrew's short fingers are in sharp contrast to the long fingers of his wife, Susan.

Often it is the little things that cumulatively and insidiously ruin our relationships. In this case, with a little effort, both Andrew and Susan learned to accommodate each other's extremes. Susan became more prompt, while Andrew learned to be less frantic. In finding a middle ground, they both benefited.

THE THUMB, AFFIRMATION OF INDIVIDUALITY

Extending from Venus, the mount of love, the thumb shows your ability to give conscious expression to your love. It also shows the expression of your individuality. In order to love others, you must first know and love yourself.

The thumb consists of two phalanxes—will and logic. The ideal thumb reaches the middle of the tamas phalanx of Jupiter, and the phalanxes of will and logic are equal in length and width.

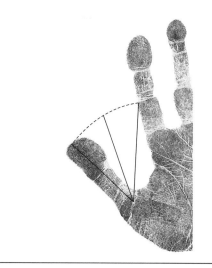

A long thumb reveals an independent, dynamic, and outgoing nature.

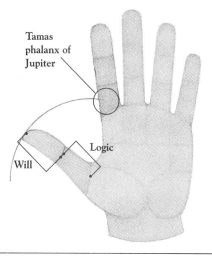

The thumb shows the expression of your individuality.

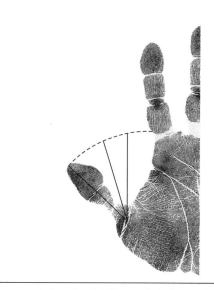

A short thumb indicates a lack of motivation.

LONG THUMB

A long thumb reveals your independent, dynamic, and outgoing nature. You have a great wish to achieve success and a desire to express your individuality.

SHORT THUMB

A short thumb may indicate a lack of motivation. The short thumb formation depicts a fearful disposition easily swayed by the views of others. You need to guard against inhibitions and feelings of uncertainty. You tend to misinterpret a well-intentioned suggestion as a criticism or threat.

You can gain inspiration from the biographies of highly motivated persons, who may serve as role models. Realizing that many of your fears stem from your dread of the unknown, you can learn to build courage and confidence through new positive experiences.

BALANCED WILL AND LOGIC PHALANXES

Ideally, the two phalanxes of will and logic are equal in length. The ability to act (will) based upon sound reasoning (logic) allows you to express yourself objectively.

SHORT WILL AND LONG LOGIC

Although you may have the ability to realize your ambitions, you lack the willpower to accomplish these goals.

You may also use your highly developed logic to rationalize your lack of initiative. You may excuse your lack of achievement by blaming circumstances or other people. You have a tendency to be rigid and defensive. Excessive reasoning to justify your way of seeing things can be detrimental to a healthy relationship. You should make a conscious effort to become more flexible in your attitudes and to develop empathy for your partner. Perhaps you can become involved in a worthwhile community activity.

LONG WILL AND SHORT LOGIC

You have a strong-willed, obstinate, and domineering temperament. Because you do not take the time to consider the implications of your actions, you can be inconsiderate. Your headstrong nature may cause difficulties in a relationship as you have a tendency to impose your will on your partner without listening to his or her needs.

By taking the time to reflect on how your impulsive and willful behavior has created mis-

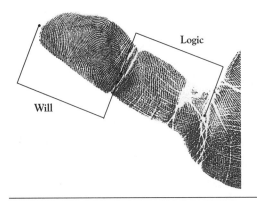

Ideally, the two phalanxes of will and logic are equal in length.

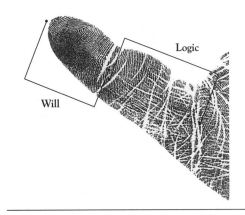

This combination shows a possible lack of willpower needed to accomplish goals.

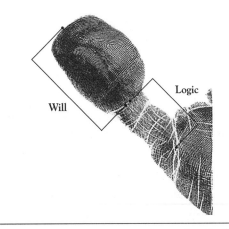

This combination shows a tendency to be self-willed and obstinate.

understandings with others in the past, you can learn to refrain from forming quick opinions.

Jeremy: The Attention-Seeker

Jeremy believed that his mother preferred his older brother over him. In his envy, he smashed his mother's favorite antique vase, then hid the pieces in his brother's room so that he would be blamed. Jeremy's desire for his mother's affection eclipsed the fact that she would be heartbroken to lose her favorite vase. His faulty reasoning is indicated by his short logic phalanx.

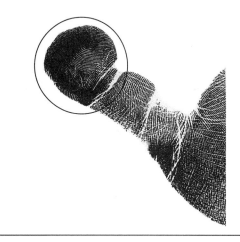

A clublike formation on the will phalanx indicates an extremely volatile personality.

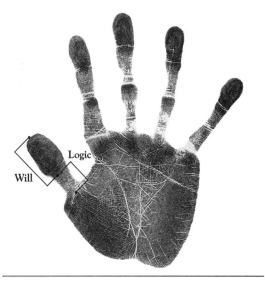

Jeremy's faulty reasoning is indicated by his short logic phalanx.

CLUBBED THUMB FORMATION

A clublike formation on the will phalanx indicates an extremely volatile personality. You may be extremely individualistic, subjective, and defensive. Although you may appear outwardly calm, an unreasonable, possibly abusive and vengeful temperament may break forth under stress. Under these circumstances, it is difficult for your relationship to flourish.

Recognizing your tendency to overreact to others, you should seek appropriate advice in order to come to terms with your hidden anger.

BALANCED-ANGLED THUMB

The relationship of the thumb to the rest of the fingers when your hands are in normal resting position—as when your hand prints are being

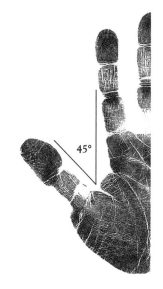

A balanced-angled thumb indicates spontaneity and expressiveness.

taken—shows the degree to which you are open or inhibited in your self-expression. Ideally, the thumb and the Jupiter finger form an angle of 45 degrees. This balanced angle shows that you are open and spontaneous in expressing yourself. In your relationships you take the feelings of your partner into consideration.

NARROW-ANGLED THUMB

A held-in thumb shows that you feel inhibited and perhaps preoccupied with your inability to cope with challenging circumstances. You may have a constant fear of the unknown or unfamiliar, and you find it difficult to open up. You tend to lack faith in yourself, and are unable to trust your intuition. Consequently, you seek relationships that provide you with a feeling of security.

Over time, your tendency to be overly dependent on your partner can harm your relationship. You need, therefore, to talk openly and honestly about your feelings with your partner. If you make a conscious effort to become self-reliant by accomplishing modest tasks, you can learn to become more confident. As you overcome your fears, you are better prepared to undertake life's challenges.

WIDE-ANGLED THUMB

A wide-angled thumb shows that you are very expressive. However, in your spontaneity and exuberance you may be inconsiderate of how others feel. You must exercise self-restraint in your relationships; otherwise, your excessive enthusiasm may overwhelm and alienate your partner. You must also guard against taxing your own energy.

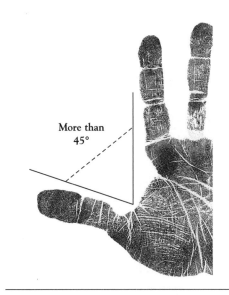

A wide-angled thumb indicates a necessity to exercise self-restraint.

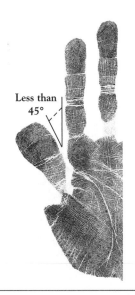

A held-in thumb indicates inhibition.

NAILS, ARMOR OF THE NERVOUS SYSTEM

Nails are an especially significant feature of the hand, as they are nature's way of protecting the nerve endings. Nails reflect your stamina and ability to cope with stress; therefore, the condition of your nails may indicate the degree to which the state of your nervous system affects your relationships.

BROAD NAILS

Broad nails show that you are open-minded, tolerant, and relaxed. You have an easygoing nature capable of absorbing stress. Broad nails denote a healthy nervous system and physical vitality. You have good circulation; you are resourceful and optimistic in your approach to life. You believe in extending yourself to others unconditionally. Although basically endowed with an excellent physical constitution, you must be careful not to exhaust yourself. You have a tendency to go to extremes: you accept all that life has to offer with enthusiasm, and also good-naturedly take on all that others ask of you.

LONG, NARROW NAILS

The long, narrow nail speaks of grace, refinement, and a strong aesthetic sense. You may be idealistic in your desire for the perfect relationship. You need to develop more tolerance and patience regarding your expectations of others.

Generally, this nail will be seen in conjunction with fine texture on the hand. Often you will gravitate toward professions that do not require strenuous physical exertion, and that give your aesthetic sense full expression.

FLARED NAILS

Flared nails indicate an extremely analytical nature. You often have the same desire to share and accomplish as does the broad-nail type. However, the short length of the nail and its nar-

A broad nail.

A long, narrow nail.

A flared nail.

row base suggest that you lack the nervous resistance to carry out your actions in a calm, relaxed manner. You may become nervous over slight disagreements. You can be easily upset, defensive, and prone to nervous strain. Your high-strung nature makes you vulnerable to all sorts of anxieties and impatient outbursts, which exhaust you.

Your energy can best be exercised in research activities or other detailed work. You should make a conscious effort to avoid being overcritical. You need to curb the tendency to find faults in your partner, which can place a strain on your relationship.

SHORT NAILS

Short, squarish nails reveal an extremely nervous disposition that is prone to temperamental and unpredictable behavior. You are analytical, with a tendency toward perfectionism. You can easily become intolerant of those who fail to measure up to your critical standards.

You must guard against losing your cool during disagreements and learn to see things from a larger perspective. If you are too fastidious, you may annoy your partner.

A short, squarish nail.

BITTEN NAILS

Bitten nails indicate that you have a nervous temperament. Biting your nails destroys the very armor that protects your nervous system. You need to learn to recognize what triggers this habit. Then you can find a harmless alternative for relieving tension: for example, counting to ten, deep breathing, or drinking a tall glass of water. Such a diversion may give you the time to calm down and perceive your situation more clearly.

THE MAJOR LINES: INDICATIONS OF COMPATIBILITY

Certain formations of each of the major lines are significant indicators of your ability to develop positive relationships.

HEAD LINE AND LIFE LINE

The head line shows your ability to apply reason in your everyday patterns of behavior (see "The Quadrangle: Landing Strip of the Angels," chapter 2). The life line indicates the state of your health, and your approach toward life. Ideally these lines should originate at a slight distance from each other, indicating an appropriate resonance between thinking and action.

HEAD LINE JOINED TO LIFE LINE

The joined origin of the head and life lines is considered to be a sign of wisdom. This formation indicates that you have an extremely sensi-

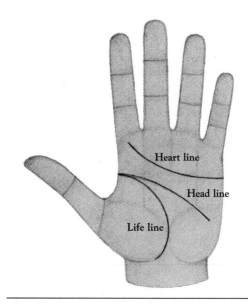

The major lines.

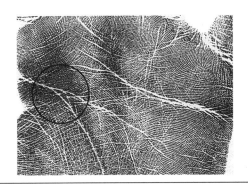

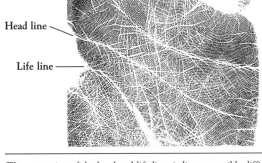

The head line joined to the life line indicates an extremely sensitive nature.

The separation of the head and life lines indicates possible difficulty in finding balance between thoughts and actions.

tive nature. During the period of your life when the lines are joined, you may feel as if you are "walking on hot coals." Until you reach the age when the lines separate, you may be in a constant state of introspection and self-questioning. At the same time you may feel restricted in your self-expression.

The separation of the head and life lines indicates a sense of freedom. You are learning to distance yourself from your acute sensitivity and, instead, transform this energy into empathy for others. This formation indicates your ability to be successful in the healing professions. In your relationships, your sensitivity can be a great asset in helping you to respond to the needs of others; however, you need to guard against the tendency to be overwhelmed by your emotions.

HEAD LINE WIDELY SEPARATED FROM LIFE LINE

The head and life lines with widely separate origins indicate that you may have difficulty finding a balance between your thoughts and actions. Although you have lofty ideals, shown by the proximity of your head line to your heart line, they may not be grounded in objective

reality. You are unable to channel your carefree and independent thinking in a disciplined and structured manner. You have a tendency to be insensitive in your relationships. You lack empathy, and in your intensity and enthusiasm disregard the feelings of those close to you. You also tend to demand appreciation and recognition from others.

You need to make a conscious attempt to develop consideration for others and allow yourself to feel tenderness and gentleness in your heart.

Carlo and Pam: Sensitivity Meets Independence

When your head-line origin corresponds to your partner's line, you are likely to have a similar approach to life and, consequently, can easily identify with each other's point of view. This is not always a requirement for a successful relationship, of course. For example, Carlo and Pam have remained friends for over thirty years, despite having very different life- and head-line origins: one is joined, the other is separate. This has caused some difficulty in their relationship, as Pam's impulsive and adventurous nature is at odds with Carlo's more cautious temperament, which she finds frustrating. Nevertheless, they have learned to turn their difference into an

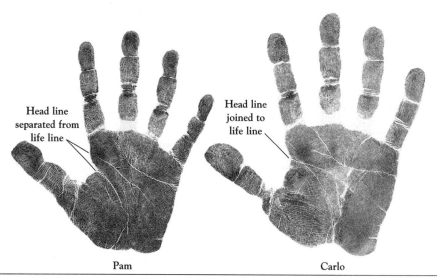

Head line
separated from
life line

Head line
joined to
life line

Pam   Carlo

Carlo centers and calms Pam and helps her focus her energies, while she encourages him to try new things.

advantage. Carlo centers and calms Pam and helps her focus her energies, while she encourages him to try new things.

Neil and Chris: Compatible Twins

These twin brothers are also best friends and together have opened their own thriving computer business. Note the similarity in their head-line origins.

SHORT HEAD LINE

A head line ending in Rahu, the mount related to the present environment, indicates that your focus may be limited to immediate concerns. You have a tendency to believe that you can only realize your ideals if you have money or visible signs of security. You may have a miserly attitude toward business matters. You may also seek out a companion who can satisfy your material needs.

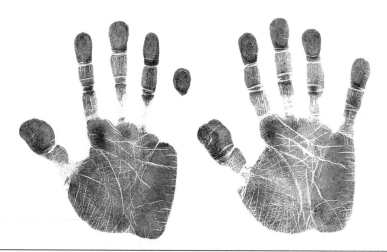

Similar head-line origins in twin brothers Neil and Chris.

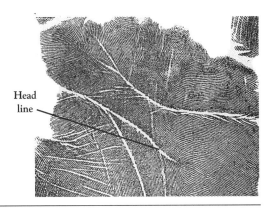

Head
line

A short head line indicates that focus may be limited to immediate concerns.

You need to learn to redirect your focus away from the need for immediate security toward a broader vision of life. You should make a conscious effort to incorporate some of the more intangible pleasures into your life. Meditation and yoga may be useful in learning how to grow your head line.

Melissa: Letting Go of the Past

Melissa, a cardiologist, fell in love with Kyle, her patient. Unfortunately, he did not return her love. Unable to see beyond her disappointment and learn from the experience, she became sick from anger and resentment. Her short head line indicates that she temporarily closed herself to the possibility of developing a mutually satisfying relationship with someone else.

LONG, STRAIGHT HEAD LINE TO MARS POSITIVE

The ideal head-line termination is at the border of Mars positive and Luna. When you combine the energy and passion of Mars positive with the sensitivity and creativity of Luna, you believe miracles can happen.

A long, straight head line ending on Mars positive, however, reveals an overly intellectual attitude toward life. You tend to be headstrong, intense, unyielding, and self-justifying. You rationalize everything in your relationships. Although your strength of purpose may prove successful in fighting for what you believe, your single-mindedness may be detrimental to your relationships.

You should make a conscious effort to empathize with your partner and encourage the sharing of feelings.

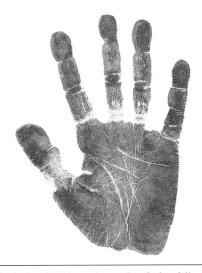

Melissa's short head line indicates that she has difficulty seeing beyond her immediate situation.

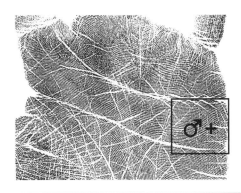

A long, straight head line to Mars positive reveals an overly intellectual attitude toward life.

Derek and Elsie: Shiva and Shakti

Derek's straight head line to Mars positive indicates his abrupt, intense manner. Elsie's head line to Luna reflects her idealistic, sensitive nature. Her aesthetic and artistic temperament complements his passionate nature. However, at times his direct manner hurts her feelings, causing tension between them.

Sarah: Change by Wisdom or Experience

Jerry's wife had been in a coma for many years when Sarah fell in love with him. Although she wanted them to live together, Jerry asked her to be understanding and supportive of his decision to remain fully committed to the care of his wife. She was unable to realize that Jerry's loyalty to his wife was an indication of his profound spirit. Jerry also loved Sarah deeply, but she resented his unwillingness to live with her and nagged him constantly. Her straight head line indicates her unyielding temperament at that time.

It was only when he died shortly after his wife that Sarah came to understand the depth of Jerry's friendship and love for her. She was so moved by this realization that her heart melted. She became more loving and gentle and her head line began to curve.

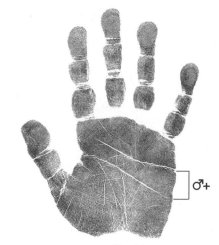

Derek

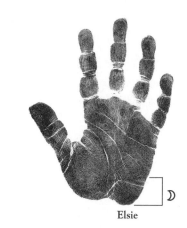

Elsie

Elsie's aesthetic temperament complements Derek's passionate nature.

 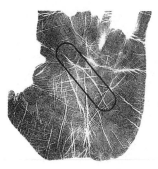

Before   **After**

In these prints, Sarah's head line has gone from straight to curved.

LIFE LINE FORMATIONS

The formation of the life line shows your motivation to live a harmonious existence. People often associate this line with how long they are going to live; however, it has more to do with the quality of your life. If you recognize that you are able to subtly program your enthusiasm for living, you can grow a longer life line.

Sabrina: Building a New Life

A comparison between these two prints shows that Sabrina's life line has grown. When the first print was taken, Sabrina was feeling emotionally distraught due to the recent breakup of her marriage. She had lost her sense of direction. The second hand print, taken two years later, reveals her renewed inspiration for living. She found a satisfying and challenging new career in teaching. With her more stable lifestyle, Sabrina became more self-reliant and less emotionally fragile.

Jeff and Tracy: Breaking the Cycle

Jeff and his daughter Tracy are learning to work out issues of the heart. In his active left hand, Jeff has an ideal life line, indicating a desire for harmony. In his inactive hand, however, he has a straight life line, showing a subconscious tendency to attract difficult circumstances. His daughter Tracy has a straight life line in her active (right) hand, indicating a conscious tendency to create conflict. Jeff realizes that his daughter has the potential to trigger his subconscious patterns of negative behavior. By learning to deal with his own propensity to engage in conflict, he is now better able to help his daughter develop a more appropriate approach to life.

BALANCED LIFE LINE

A round, healthy life line encircling the mount of Venus indicates a natural inclination to live harmoniously. The round life line indicates that you are stable and self-contained, with a strong likelihood of being able to make a commitment in a relationship.

LIFE LINE TO LUNA

A life line traveling toward the mount of Luna shows that your mental and physical energy can be dissipated. You have a tendency to be easily distracted by your sensory impressions and, with no clear priorities, you may become restless and

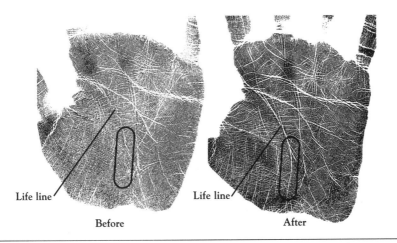

Life line   Life line

Before   **After**

A comparison between these two prints shows that Sabrina's life line has grown.

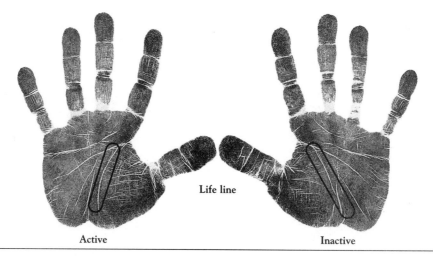

Active   **Life line**   Inactive

Although Jeff desires harmony, he has a subconscious tendency to attract difficult circumstances.

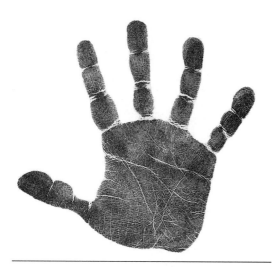

Complexities in Tracy's active hand indicate a conscious tendency to create conflict.

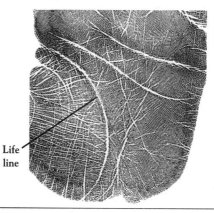

Life line

A round, healthy life line encircling the mount of Venus indicates a natural inclination to live harmoniously.

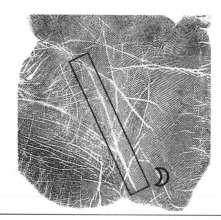

A life line traveling toward the mount of Luna shows that mental and physical energy can be dissipated.

dissatisfied. Although enthusiastic about accomplishing numerous goals, you may be somewhat unfocused and disorganized. Consequently, your energy may dissipate, leaving you feeling exhausted. You may have difficulty being committed to a long-term relationship.

Awareness of your own behavior patterns is the key to positive change. Learning to focus on whatever you are doing, or whomever you are with, brings stability to your life.

THE IMPORTANCE OF CHECKING BOTH HANDS

We often call our partner our better half; yet in reality, we are simply looking at the reflection of our own subconscious in the other person. When we attract someone into our life, we are asking to be shown this hidden side that, on a conscious level, we would have difficulty seeing. Often a marriage or other close relationship begins to deteriorate as we avoid looking at this reflection. It may be too difficult to face our imperfections and make the necessary changes to improve. We can easily put the blame on our partner, our mirror. We may even move on to someone else only to discover another reflection of ourself. By recognizing our limitations, as well as our strengths, we can help ourself and our partner to grow.

Ernst and Nina: Your Partner As Your Mirror

These are the prints of a healer and his wife. Ernst's healing ability is shown by healing stigmata, a beautiful quadrangle, and a destiny line originating on Luna. His wife, Nina, has a short head line in her active hand, indicating her need to be financially secure. However, Nina has

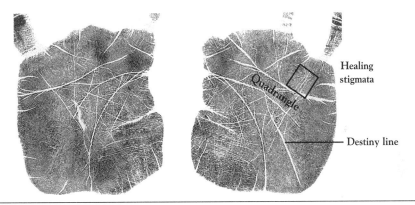

Ernst's (left) inactive and (right) active hands.

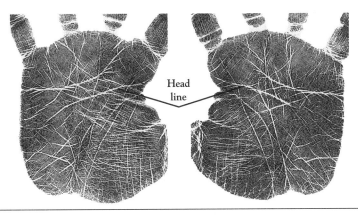

Nina's (left) inactive and (right) active hands.

an ideal head line in her left hand. She understands her husband's dedication to his vocation despite her anxiety over money. The short head line in Ernst's inactive hand shows that, at times, he will question his own motivation to work selflessly for others.

Nature has brought them together to test their ability to evolve and grow. Who's active hand will bring out the negative or positive tendencies carried over from the other's past lives? Nina will test Ernst's commitment to remain a healer; Ernst will challenge Nina's willingness to allow her humanitarian nature to surface.

LOVE IN THE MAKING: RECREATING OUR RELATIONSHIPS

Often we find ourselves repeating negative patterns of behavior. We may be drawn to people who bring us unhappiness; we may be dissatisfied with our jobs; or we may persist in unproductive ways of thinking that create pessimism and negativity. We may want to change, but are uncertain about how to proceed. Sometimes we tell ourselves that we are just unlucky. We may even blame other people or life itself for our misfortune. In our pain, we ask, "Why is this happening to me?"

In reality, this may be a very good question. We cannot change what has already happened, but we have a choice about how we perpetuate the effects in our life. It is possible to break negative patterns. The first step is to recognize that a pattern exists. Then we can examine the circumstances in our life that gave rise to our attracting harmful situations. During this process we learn

Love in the making.

to accept responsibility for the direction of our life. No matter what tendencies we are born with, we need not be affected by them throughout our whole life. We have the free will to change.

As the Sanskrit verse says, "Yesterday is only a dream and tomorrow is only a vision; but today, well-lived, makes every yesterday a dream of happiness and every tomorrow a vision of hope."

SEVEN STEPS TO HARMONIOUS LIVING

What concrete steps can you take to bring about positive changes? You must be patient and diligent. It takes time—as much as seven years—before a conscious mode of behavior filters into

The seven steps to harmonious living.

your subconscious and becomes automatic.

By understanding the implications of the following sequence of steps, you can teach yourself to exercise your free will constructively.

BREATH

It is your breathing that gives birth to your thoughts. The breath, without which you cannot even exist, is necessary to transform an idea into a living reality. Deep breathing indicates healthy lungs, which in turn manufacture prana, the subtle form of breath or life force, responsible for giving you strength and energy.

THOUGHT

Deep, balanced breathing—in which the cycle of inhalation and exhalation is effortless—creates a state of inner calm in which clear, objective thinking can occur. You can become more focused on the immediate issue without losing sight of the greater context.

ACTION

Once you are able to think clearly about a situation or problem, you will know how to act. You will be able to discriminate between what you want and what you need, between attraction and love, and between what is really good for you and what is not.

HABIT

Repeated appropriate actions create a positive habit. While these actions may require conscious effort at first, over time they become second nature.

CHARACTER

Habits provide the foundation of your character. Once a series of repeated actions becomes unconscious habit, you realize that you have begun to change your past tendencies.

BEHAVIOR

Your behavior reflects the changes in your character. Others will perceive you as wiser and more loving.

CIRCUMSTANCES

With a more positive attitude and behavior, the circumstances of your life will improve. You'll find greater harmony in your work, in your personal relationships, and in your spiritual life.

TECHNIQUES FOR POSITIVE CHANGE

Since proper breathing is the foundation for changes in attitudes and behavior, which in turn allow you to attract positive circumstances into your life, you should examine some basic techniques.

YOGIC BREATHING

Most of us do not breathe deeply enough. Start by breathing deeply into the belly, allowing the breath to fill the chest and lungs. Allow the breath to exhale as deeply, following the pattern of inhalation.

MASSAGE

A brisk massage of the body with mustard and sandalwood oils is invigorating and a sure way to stimulate circulation. Massage helps to relieve tension in the body, enabling you to breathe more deeply.

MEDITATION

Meditation also helps you breathe properly. Sit in a comfortable position with the spine erect, preferably facing east. Sitting this way allows the spinal centers to be aligned, which permits the life currents to flow more easily. Your breathing becomes calm and your concentration is enhanced. By concentrating on the point between the eyebrows with closed eyes, you will be able to visualize a white light. Gradually, you

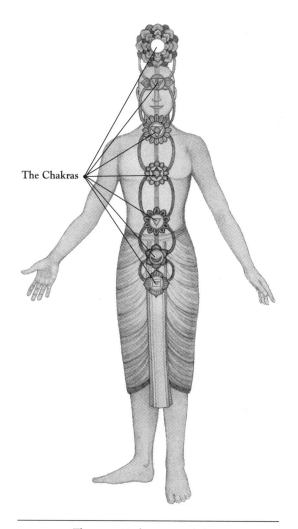

The Chakras

The seven spinal centers or chakras.

withdraw from the senses of taste, touch, sight, smell, and hearing. This process, in turn, slows down the breathing and relaxes the heart, enabling you to achieve a calm state of mind.

If you view any object through a prism in daylight, you can easily see that everything has its own color vibration. The universe within each of us also has this prismatic effect, as each spinal center or chakra corresponds to a different color of the rainbow. By concentrating on the light within, you can activate the entire spectrum of color from the root chakra to the crown center. This process marks the beginning of a joyous connection with the soul. As color is fused into the luminance and purity of light, so you also melt into the radiance of spirit. In this exalted state of being, all blockages are removed. In this calmness, broadcasting your heartfelt wish out into the cosmos serves as a soul call to that universal intelligence that is primarily responsible for helping you materialize the very thing you desire.

VISUALIZATION

Visualization is a technique that can be used to grow positive lines and signs in the hand. For example, if you wish to grow your heart line, you should gaze at both hands when you wake up. Look at the left first, then the right, and mentally visualize a nice curved heart line. At first, it might only be wishful thinking. Imagine that the heart line is rising with a nice curve onto the Jupiter mount; then steadily go over the entire heart line, visualizing it more clearly as clean and smooth. Follow it mentally all the way from Jupiter to its termination at the base of the mount of Mercury.

In order to increase the benefits of visualization, it is always good to rub both hands together before starting the exercise. This gets the circulation going, stimulating the two-way traffic of nerve impulses traveling to the fingertips and back again to the brain. Then massage each finger with a slight twisting motion, energizing the element each finger represents. Start with the little finger and move toward the thumb. In this way, you activate all the elements—beginning with ether, then air, fire, water, and ending with earth. Since prenatal traits are seen in the inactive hand and postnatal in the active, make sure to massage the fingers of both hands. Usually it takes about three months of consistent practice to notice change in various lines and signs in the hands.

Conclusion

The spirit gives birth to the mind and body and not the other way around. Looking after your spiritual needs automatically encompasses all your other needs. When your heart is filled with complete confidence, when you believe from the depths of your being that what you are contemplating is your birthright, and when you have trust in the divine law of "cause and effect," then something magical happens.

Sincerity, attentiveness, selfless sacrifice, even-mindedness and, above all, loyalty, play an essential role in all your interpersonal relationships. Once you have managed to attract the person who is rightfully your partner, you should never take that person for granted or relax your attention, care, and concern. The foundation for a lasting relationship is the gift of self-sacrifice and the capacity to surrender to each other's needs.

The great Himalayan saint Babaji once said, "Banat, Banat, Ban Jai," which translates as "By doing, doing, it is done." What an assurance from a divine guru! It is comforting to know that we have the power to change ourselves for the better, and our relationships in the process.

I have tried to offer many practical techniques in this book to help readers on the way to an open, expansive, loving, and sharing relationship. It is a great privilege for me to share in the quest to cultivate meaningful relationships by examining the implications of the lines and signs of the hand that reflect our ability to love.

May joyous blessings be with us all.

Twelve Key Points to Remember

It may be helpful to remember the following points as you go about your daily activities. There will come a time when you are no longer just testing these ideas. Your whole being will have assimilated them. Your magnetic range will change and you will find yourself forming healthier and happier relationships.

1. Love is native to the soul.
2. Your interpersonal relationships are the result of your magnetic range.
3. Objective self-analysis, through the study of the lines and signs of the hand, is the key to understanding the difference between your needs and your desires.
4. To develop a better heart line and other positive signs you must be willing to change your own thought patterns. The quality of a line is in direct proportion to the quality of thought that creates it.
5. Remember the importance of developing your sattwic qualities. By learning to become calm, loving, trustworthy, and dependable, you can attract positive relationships and guard against harmful associations.
6. A happy, healthy, and successful life depends on harmonious thought patterns. "As we think, so we are."
7. Even though your life is governed to a great extent by prenatal karmic compulsions, remember that you have the power of free will to create new patterns of behavior.
8. Develop harmony in the three gunas—sattwa, rajas, and tamas. This will cause a more balanced flow of energy that will refine your magnetic range.
9. Recognize that overidentification with the physical world of tamas leads to

disillusionment. By embracing sattwa, you can perform miracles.

10. Moodiness destroys your personal magnetism.

11. By being open to recognizing that negative patterns of behavior may spring from inappropriate thinking, you can begin to effect positive change. You should not be afraid to seek objective guidance.

12. Remind yourself of the age-old saying, "Live for your friend, and your friend will live for you."

Prayer of Saint Francis of Assisi

Lord, make me an instrument of your peace.

Where there is hatred, let me sow Love;

Where there is injury—pardon;

Where there is doubt—faith;

Where there is despair—hope;

Where there is darkness—light;

And where there is sadness—joy.

Lord, grant that I may seek to comfort rather
than to be comforted,

to understand rather than to be understood,

to love rather than to be loved.

For it is by giving that one receives,

by forgiving that one is forgiven,

and by dying that one awakens to eternal life.

Index of Case Histories

Index

Taking an Impression of Your Hands

The back pocket of this book contains one inked acetate sheet, sufficient for taking a print of each hand. Below are instructions for taking an impression of your hands. These prints will allow you to see details that may be difficult to discern from your actual palm. Use the information and the diagrams found in the book to determine your strengths and potential problem areas.

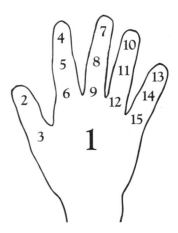

1. Prepare a large, clear surface (i.e., kitchen counter or table) and cover the area with newspaper. Have soap, paper towels, and a sink nearby for cleanup after taking prints. **Important:** For better clarity, *do not* wash hands before printing.

Remove wristwatch and any jewelry from hands and wrists, roll up long sleeves, and wear an apron or otherwise protect clothing.

2. Carefully separate the two layers of the inked acetate sheet. Place each layer down flat, inked sides up, on a section of newspaper. (Setting the sheets on a section of newspaper will provide enough surface "give" to ensure thorough hand-to-ink contact and give a complete print, including the center of the palm.) Place a blank sheet of paper next to the acetate sheets, also on top of a section of newspaper.

3. To take a print of each hand, begin with your right hand. Place your right palm down on one of the inked sheets, holding it still, yet relaxed and without any tension, to avoid smudging.

4. Use your left hand to press firmly down onto the parts of your right hand according to the numerical sequence shown in the diagram.

5. Use your left hand to hold down the edges of the acetate sheet, then lift your right hand in one clean motion. Place your inked, right hand down on the blank sheet of paper, hold your right hand still, and again press it with your left hand in the same numerical sequence as used earlier for inking.

When finished, use your left hand to hold down the edges of the paper and quickly lift up your right hand.

6. *Do not* wash your hands yet. You will want to complete the printing process and have a finished print of each hand, so tolerate ink on the back of one hand for a bit so as not to interfere with the printing process.

7. Now repeat the entire process using your left hand.

8. When done, clean up using more soap than water. With patience, all the ink will come off.

Now you have a print of each hand with which to consult the diagrams and information in the book regarding your own strengths and potential problem areas.